Monsters

Discovering Mythology

**Other titles in Lucent Books
Discovering Mythology Series include:**

Death and the Underworld
Gods and Goddesses
Heros
Quests and Journeys

Monsters

Discovering Mythology

by Don Nardo

Lucent Books, Inc.
P.O. Box 289011, San Diego, California

On cover: Perseus holding the head of Medusa

Library of Congress Cataloging-in-Publication Data

Nardo, Don, 1947–
    Monsters / by Don Nardo.
        p. cm. — (Discovering mythology)
Includes bibliographical references and index.
    ISBN 1-56006-853-1 (lib : alk. paper)
    1. Monsters—Juvenile literature. 2. Mythology—Juvenile
literature. [1. Monsters. 2. Mythology.] I. Title. II. Series.
    GR825 .N37 2002
    398.2'1—dc21

00-012949

Printed in the U.S.A.

Contents

Foreword

Created by ancient cultures, the world's many and varied mythologies are humanity's attempt to make sense of otherwise inexplicable phenomena. Floods, drought, death, creation, evil, even the possession of knowledge—all have been explained in myth. The ancient Greeks, for example, observed the different seasons but did not understand why they changed. As a result, they reasoned that winter, a cold, dark time of year, was the result of a mother in mourning; the three months of winter were the days the goddess Demeter missed her daughter Persephone who had been tricked into spending part of her year in the underworld. Likewise, the people of India experienced recurring droughts, weeks and months during which their crops withered and their families starved. To explain the droughts, the Indians created the story of Vritra, a terrible demon who lived in the clouds and sucked up all the world's moisture. And the Vikings, in their search for an understanding of wisdom and knowledge, created Odin, their culture's most powerful god, who gave the world the gift of poetry and possessed two mythic ravens named Thought and Memory.

The idea of myth, fantastic stories that answer some of humanity's most enduring questions, spans time, distance, and differing cultural ideologies. Humans—whether living in the jungles of South America, along the rocky coasts of northern Europe, or on the islands of Japan—all formulated stories in an attempt to understand their world. And although their worlds differed greatly, they sometimes found similar ways of explaining the unknown or unexplainable events of their lives. Other times, there were differences, but the method of explanation—the myth—remains the same.

Each book in the Discovering Mythology series revolves around a specific topic—for example, death and the underworld; monsters; or heroes—and each chapter examines a selection of myths related to that topic. This allows young readers to note both the similarities and differences across cultures and time. Almost all cultures have myths to explain creation and death, for instance, but the actual stories sometimes vary widely. The Babylonians believed that the earth was the offspring of primordial parents, while the Navajo Indians of North America assert that the world emerged over time much like an infant grows into an adult. In ancient Greek mythology, a deceased person passed quickly into the underworld, a physical place that offered neither reward nor punishment for one's deeds in life. Egyptian myths, on the other hand, contended that a person's quality of existence in the afterlife, an ambiguous state of being, depended on his actions on earth.

In other cases, the symbolic creature or hero and what it represents are the same, but the purpose of the story may be different. Although monster myths in different cultures may not always explain the same phenomenon or offer insight into the same ethical quandary, monsters nearly always represent evil. The shape-shifting beast-men of ancient Africa represented the evils of trickery and wile. These vicious animal-like creatures transformed themselves into attractive, charming humans to entrap unsuspecting locals. Persia's White Demon devoured townspeople and nobles alike; it took the intelligence and strength of an extraordinary prince to defeat the monster and save the countryside. Even the Greek Furies, although committing their evil acts in the name of justice, were ugly, violent creatures who murdered people guilty of killing others. Only the goddess Athena could tame them.

The Discovering Mythology series presents the myths of many cultures in a format accessible to young readers. Fully documented secondary source quotes and numerous mythological tales enliven the text. Sidebars highlight interesting stories, creatures, and traditions. Annotated bibliographies offer ideas for further research. Each book in this engaging series provides students with a wealth of information as well as launching points for further discussion.

The Dragons of the Past

All through the nineteenth and twentieth centuries, monsters of every description terrified the world. A giant with green skin and bolts through its neck, which had been created in a laboratory by a German scientist, escaped and murdered several people; an Egyptian pharaoh who had been dead for three thousand years came to life and went on a rampage; a two-hundred-foot-tall lizard and a giant moth repeatedly destroyed Tokyo and other Japanese cities; a huge ape ran amok in New York City until airplanes shot it off the Empire State Building; giant ants infested the storm drains of Los Angeles; a sulfur-eating creature from the planet Venus killed hundreds of people in Rome and wrecked what was left of the Colosseum; a colony of werewolves took over a New England town; and a race of emotionless beings who had hatched from large seed pods almost eradicated the human race.

Modern Monster Myths

These and countless other bizarre and dangerous monsters, of course, are figments of the imaginations of writers and filmmakers. The creatures described—Frankenstein's monster, the Mummy, Godzilla, King Kong, and the rest—can still be seen haunting television screens; and each year numerous other such denizens of doom are created for movies, television, novels, short stories, comic books, video games, and so on. Collectively, they represent a modern monster mythos—that is, a collection of mythical creatures, each existing within its own fantasy world, and occupying a niche within the greater public consciousness.

Why did the modern world create its own popular mythology populated by fantastic, frightening, and threatening creatures? In the larger sense, the answer lies partly in the fact that human beings of every race and culture have always developed their own local mythologies.

In the past, especially before the rise of modern science, these collections of stories most often developed as a means of explaining the wonders of nature as well as human nature. As modern mythologist Max J. Herzberg puts it, people in past ages were puzzled by many questions, including

> the origin of fire, the fashion in which various animals and plants

came to be, the reasons for one man's prosperity and another man's troubles, the nature of death and the problem of an afterworld. To answer questions such as these the men of ancient days devised myths.[1]

Because they had not yet developed the scientific means and knowledge to map and explain the world, the ancients were

Godzilla, one of the most famous denizens of the modern monster mythos, confronts an array of human artillery, which of course fails to kill him.

The head of the Greek monster Medusa, whose gaze was said to turn people to stone, lies severed in this drawing based on a work by Leonardo da Vinci.

also afraid of what might be lurking in the dark, under the ground, in caves, or in uncharted lands or seas. So they envisioned a host of monsters—giants, demons, dragons, three-headed dogs, snake-haired women, shape-shifters, and the like—inhabiting these places.

Later, as knowledge and science replaced fear and ignorance, these monsters and their stories became quaint, entertaining relics of vanished cultures. Yet despite their ever-growing store of scientific, factual knowledge about the world and how it works, modern humans did not outgrow their need to express and relieve their deep-seated fears and anxieties nor their need to be entertained. So

they invented their own mythical monsters. The difference is that the modern versions are often either created by scientists or are the unintended results of meddling by scientists (for example, Dr. Frankenstein's monster being pieced together in a lab or radiation from nuclear blasts causing insects, lizards, and humans to grow into giants and become killers). Moreover, these monsters are also destroyed by scientifically created means (tanks, flamethrowers, atom bombs, lab-engineered microbes, ray guns, and the like). In the language of modern myth, then, science is both potentially dangerous and heroic since it can make monsters and also kill them.

Ancient Monsters and Heroes

In the mythologies of the ancients, by contrast, the monsters were almost always killed by human heroes using either their bare hands and wits or simple weapons such as clubs, swords, and spears. In fact, the confrontation between the monster on a more or less equal footing was key. "The mythical monster is present in any number of shapes," the world-famous mythologist Edith Hamilton once wrote,

In this painting on an ancient Greek cup, the hero Cadmus, founder of the city of Thebes, kills a monstrous serpent.

"but they are there only to give the hero his reward of glory. What could a hero do in a world without them? They are always overcome by him."[2]

The question, of course, as recalled by the old adage about the chicken and the egg, is which came first—the monster or the hero? The conclusive answer to that question is lost in the mists of time. However, some modern scholars have offered tentative theories, one of the most interesting of them put forth in the 1970s by the late, great scientist Carl Sagan. He pointed out that many ancient cultures, often separated from one another by oceans and other formidable barriers, developed very similar images for their mythical monsters. In particular, almost all cultures pictured dragons or serpents, invariably viewing them as evil and threatening. Perhaps, he suggested, buried deep in the subconscious mind of all humans, there is a racial memory of a period in the dim past when our primitive forebears had to struggle for their very existence against real monsters. "Is it only an accident," he asks in *The Dragons of Eden*,

that the common human sounds commanding silence or attracting

attention seem strangely imitative of the hissing of reptiles? Is it possible that dragons posed a problem for our proto-human ancestors of a few million years ago, and that the terror they evoked and the deaths they caused helped bring about the evolution of human intelligence? . . . Could the pervasive dreams and common fears of "monsters," which children develop shortly after they are able to talk, be evolutionary vestiges [surviving remnants] of quite adaptive . . . [survival] responses to dragons?[3]

Even if Sagan's intriguing questions cannot be answered with any assurance, it is well documented that the ancient Greeks, Egyptians, Chinese, Persians, Norse, Celts, and many others had strangely similar stories about dragons. This fact alone—that such monsters are part of the collective heritage that connects the ancestors of every person alive today—is more than enough to warrant an examination of these ancient stories. That they remain as entertaining as ever is, of course, an added bonus!

Ancient Greece: The Beast with a Woman's Face

Chapter One

The timeless stories of ancient Greek mythology are filled with incredible beings, including many monsters. Monstrous creatures, along with heroes and the Greek gods, freely roamed the world of a bygone era that the classical Greeks (Pericles, Socrates, Plato, and their fellows) referred to as the Age of Heroes. One element that unites all of the stories from this heroic age is a sense of wonder; for it was seen as a magical, more admirable time when the gods and humans regularly interacted.

The exploits of the Greek heroes often involved a confrontation with evil—usually in the form of a monster with an animal's body and a human face. Interestingly, in many cases the face was that of a woman. The reason for this is not certain, although clearly most of the classical Greek men who told and retold these myths delegated women to a lower social status than themselves. Although his rhetoric was probably on the extreme side, even for his unenlightened times, the poet Hesiod (who flourished about 700 B.C.) expressed a view of women that many men of that age probably shared. He called the first woman, the mythical Pandora, "the hopeless trap, deadly to men." From her, he says in his poem, the *Theogony*, "comes all the race of womankind, the deadly female race and tribe of wives who live with mortal men and bring them harm, no help to them in poverty but ready enough to share with them in wealth."[4] One of Hesiod's younger contemporaries, the poet Semonides, agreed, writing,

This is the worst plague Zeus [leader of the gods] has made—women. . . . The man who lives with a woman never goes through all his day in cheerfulness. . . . Each man will take care to praise his own wife and find fault with the other's; we do not realize that the fate of all of us [men] is alike.[5]

Whatever the cause of such views, the goddesses, mortal women, and various female beings and monsters of Greek mythology were nearly always portrayed in a black-and-white, "either-or" manner. Although some female characters in Greek mythology are virginal, helpful, virtuous, and/or constructive, many are portrayed as murderous, grasping, vengeful, or simply ugly—qualities the classical Greeks

The first woman (according to Greek mythology), Pandora, opens the box that will unleash a host of troubles and sorrows into the world.

saw as basic flaws in the makeup of human beings. Among these destructive female beings were the Harpies, disgusting creatures with the bodies of birds and women's faces, who stole human food or else rendered it inedible; the Gorgons, who were so hideous that anyone who looked at them turned to stone; the awful Furies, spirits of vengeance who relentlessly chased down and punished murderers and other transgressors; and the Sphinx, a fearsome monster with a woman's head and a lion's body, which terrorized the city of Thebes, (located in mainland Greece not far to the northwest of Athens.)

The Sphinx Meets Its Match

The Sphinx was itself the hideous offspring of another female beast-human hybrid, the monster Echidna, which had the upper body of a woman and the lower body of a serpent (and which lived in a dark cave beneath the earth). Echidna had mated with her own son, the two-headed dog Orthus. No one can say for sure why the Sphinx singled out Thebes among all of the other Greek cities. (In one version of the story, the goddess Hera, Zeus's wife, sent the monster to attack the city to punish the local king for kidnapping a young man she liked.) What is certain is that the people of Thebes suddenly found themselves beset by a serious crisis. The huge and frightening beast with a woman's face appeared seemingly out of nowhere and began stalking the countryside around the city.

This sculpture of the monstrous Sphinx is presently on display at Delphi, Greece.

Unlike many other monsters that lived in those days, the Sphinx did not simply attack and kill people. Instead, it would leap out at travelers, corner them, and pose them a riddle. The monster promised that if its victim could solve the riddle, it would let him or her go; if not, the Sphinx devoured the person alive, which obviously was not a pleasant fate. And because no one could solve the riddle, one Theban after another met doom in the creature's clutches, and terror gripped the city. Making matters worse for the Thebans, news came that their ruler, old King Laius, had been killed mysteriously on the roadside

15

The Weapons That Slew the Monsters

The heroes and warriors who fought the monsters of Greek mythology were based on the distant memory of the real fighters of Bronze Age Greece. Modern scholars refer to these early Greeks as Mycenaeans (after their fortress-town of Mycenae, located in southern Greece). In this tract from his colorful book, *The Legend of Odysseus*, noted scholar-artist Peter Connolly describes some of the principal weapons used by the Mycenaeans and presumably also by the mythical heroes.

The Mycenaean warrior was a spearman. He only used his sword if his spear was lost or broken. . . . Leaf-shaped spearheads were common in the late Mycenaean period [the thirteenth century B.C.]. Early Mycenaean swords were long, pointed weapons designed for thrusting and not cutting. By the thirteenth century B.C., these had been replaced by much shorter weapons. Some were still designed for thrusting, but others were intended for chopping or hacking. A new weapon had come to Greece which was to change the face of battle. It was a long, slashing weapon which originated in central Europe. Some examples are more than 80 cm [nearly three feet] long. It was probably the most successful sword ever designed. Its iron successor [introduced after the fall of the Mycenaean kingdoms, following the introduction of iron-making technology into Greece] was used by both Greeks and Romans until the third century B.C.

This ancient vase painting shows early Greek warriors thrusting their spears at centaurs, creatures half-man and half-horse.

while on his way back from visiting another city. His widow, Queen Jocasta, and all of her subjects prayed to be delivered from their misery.

The Thebans' prayers seemed answered when a stalwart and intelligent young man named Oedipus, a traveler from the city of Corinth (situated several miles south of Thebes), appeared on the scene. Oedipus was the son of Corinth's king, Polybus. The Delphic Oracle, a priestess who was thought to be a medium between humans and Apollo, the god of prophecy, had foretold that Oedipus would end up killing his own father. In an effort to keep this prediction from coming true, Oedipus decided to leave Corinth. That is how he ended up in the vicinity of Thebes.

Oedipus stopped to rest at a village not far from Thebes. There, he heard about the Sphinx and the danger it posed to everyone for miles around. He asked one of the village elders if anyone had tried to fight the monster. Several of Thebes's best and strongest young men, the elder told him, had ventured out with their spears and swords, bent on confronting and slaying it, but the outcome was always the same: The Sphinx snapped their spears in two like twigs and then tore them limb from limb. A look of determination came over Oedipus's face. He explained how, in his city, he was known for his skill as a hunter and a fighter, and he vowed to try his hand at ridding the world of the murderous beast. The people of the village were impressed with Oedipus's courage as he went looking for the Sphinx; but they

felt sorry for him, too, for they thought his chances for success were slim.

The young man made his way quietly and cautiously through the forest, and within an hour he found a set of tracks that looked like those of a lion, only much larger. These had to be the monster's tracks, the man reasoned. Sure enough, after following them for about a mile or so, Oedipus came to a clearing through which flowed a clear, cold mountain stream; crouched on the stream's bank, drinking, was a thing that looked like it had stepped out of some twisted nightmare. Its body resembled that of a lion, except that it was at least six or seven times the size of the largest lion Oedipus had ever seen. The creature also had enormous brown wings and the breasts and face of a human woman, although in place of ordinary teeth it had razor-sharp fangs protruding from beneath its upper lip.

The Sphinx must have smelled the man's scent, for it suddenly spun around and confronted Oedipus. In a raspy voice, the creature ordered the man to come closer so that it might have a better look at him. Warily, grasping his spear tightly, Oedipus approached the beast. Giving the man the once-over, the Sphinx indicated that it planned to eat him. But lest anyone should think it unsporting or unfair, it would give him a chance to avoid that fate by posing a riddle. If the man answered it correctly, the Sphinx said, he could go on his way. If not, he would soon find himself in the dark innards of the monster's belly.

A painting on a cup found in Attica, Greece, shows the wily Oedipus solving the riddle of the Sphinx.

Yet despite the dangerous predicament he was in, Oedipus was not intimidated by the creature. He challenged the Sphinx to ask its riddle and boasted that he would solve it and then kill the beast with his spear. The Sphinx registered surprise at the man's boldness, then laughed and presented the riddle. According to

the first-century B.C. Greek historian Diodorus Siculus,

This is what was set forth by the Sphinx: "What is it that is of itself two-footed, three-footed, and four-footed?" Although the others could not see through it,

Oedipus replied that the answer was "man," for as an infant man begins to move as a four-footed being [crawling on all fours], when he is grown he is two-footed, and as an old man he is three-footed, leaning upon a staff because of his weakness.[6]

On hearing Oedipus correctly solve the riddle, the Sphinx grew wide-eyed and screamed loudly. Oedipus gripped his spear and crouched, preparing to leap at the creature and strike. But then a strange thing happened. The Sphinx began shaking all over and ran in circles, crying out in despair that it had been outwitted and vanquished by a mere human. How, it asked, could it live with the shame? Evidently, the monster could

not live with the shame because as the man looked on in astonishment, it grabbed a sword left by one of its previous victims and plunged it into its own heart. With a great thud, the Sphinx's lifeless body struck the ground. (In another version, the Sphinx jumped off a cliff to its death.) Thebes was saved, and the grateful citizens welcomed Oedipus as their king. He married Queen Jocasta, had two sons by her, and there followed for them and their people many years of happiness and prosperity.[7]

The Hideous Sisters

The creatures that had spawned the Sphinx were, the Greeks believed, among the earliest beings created at the beginning of the world. Among the other early beings were the Titans, the first race

These sculpted heads from a Greek temple depict Medusa, the deadly Gorgon who killed many people with her gaze.

The Monstrous Furies

Among the most famous and feared of the female monsters of Greek mythology were the Furies (or Erinyes). Not only did these ugly, vicious beings have wings, which allowed them to fly high, far, and fast, they also carried snakes, whips, and torches to use on their victims when they caught them. The way they chose their victims was simple. The Furies devoted themselves to tracking down, mutilating, and killing murderers, especially those who had killed their own kin.

The most famous episode featuring these monsters was their pursuit of a young man named Orestes. He had killed his own mother, Clytemnestra, in revenge for her earlier murder of her husband, and Orestes's father, Agamemnon. As he stood over his mother's blood-spattered corpse, Orestes beheld something terrifying that no others present could see: the deadly Furies, who had come to torture and kill him.

The young man escaped and ran for his life. He wandered through many lands, across seas, and over mountain chains; yet the Furies relentlessly pursued him, never letting him rest. Finally, having long felt great guilt for killing his mother, Orestes journeyed to the temple of Athena in Athens and there asked the goddess to purify his sins and kill the creatures that threatened to rend him limb from limb.

Because the man had thrown himself on her mercy, the goddess accepted his plea and absolved him of his guilt; however, she did not destroy the Furies. Instead, in this healing atmosphere of mercy and forgiveness, a wondrous thing happened. Athena ordained that there had been enough killing, and she transformed the hideous and vengeful Furies into the kindly and graceful Eumenides, protectors of all who beseech the gods. By divine grace, both man and monsters were saved.

of gods, who had arisen from the union of Gaia (the earth) and Uranus (the sky). Gaia also mated with her son Nereus, producing the sea gods Phorcys and Ceto; the latter two, in turn, mated and had six monstrous female offspring. The first three, the Graeae, were, from the moment of their birth, old hags who shared a single eye and a single tooth among them. The other three sisters were the Gorgons—Stheno, Euryale, and Medusa—whose appearance was so horrifying that any animal or human who looked directly at them turned to stone. Medusa was even more hideous than her sisters. This was because Athena (the goddess of war and wisdom) had long ago turned her hair to a mass of slithering snakes as a punishment for sleeping with the sea god Poseidon inside Athena's temple.

The Gorgons lived on an island on the far edge of the known world. And many a traveler who was lost or blown off course and accidentally encountered the dreaded sisters ended up as a pillar of solid stone. For a long time, no one dared even to think about traveling to the faraway land where the Gorgons lived and attempting to kill them. To fight these creatures, went the conventional wisdom, one had to look at them; and looking at them seemed the same thing as signing one's own death warrant. In short, eliminating just one, let alone all, of the Gorgons seemed an impossible task for any human being.

In time, however, there arose a champion who possessed the special combination of physical prowess and shrewd wit that was needed to defeat the worst of the three hideous sisters—Medusa. This hero was Perseus, whose circumstances even before he was born suggested that he was destined for greatness. Myth-teller David Bellingham explains:

> Acrisius, the king of Argos [a city in southeastern Greece], had been told by an oracle that he would one day be killed by a grandson. Therefore, he arranged for his daughter Danae to be locked in a cell of bronze until she was too old to have children; one day, however, he learned that she had become miraculously pregnant. Zeus had plans for the future of Argos and had come to her one night through an air vent in the roof of the cell as a beautiful shower of gold dust. She bore a son and named him Perseus, but Acrisius had them thrown into the sea in a wooden chest. They were washed up on the island of Seriphos, where a friendly fisherman named Dictys gave them shelter. When Perseus reached manhood, Danae told him who his father was.[8]

Now, it so happened that the fisherman's brother was Polydectes, the king of Seriphos. An unsavory, overbearing character, Polydectes took a fancy to Perseus's mother, Danae, and insisted that she marry him. She refused. But the king kept badgering her until Perseus finally stepped in and warned Polydectes to break off his pursuit. Angry at being rebuffed, the king vowed to get revenge on Danae and Perseus when the chance presented itself.

The chance for revenge came much sooner than Polydectes expected. He proposed marriage to another woman, named Hippodameia, and demanded that every man on the island provide a horse that the king would present as a gift to his prospective bride. Because Perseus owned no horses, he went to Polydectes and offered to give him an alternative gift; and in the course of their conversation,

A *painting on pottery shows the hero Perseus as an infant, held by his mother Danae. Perseus's father was Zeus, leader of the Greek gods.*

they discussed the idea of Perseus bringing back a truly novel gift—the head of the Gorgon Medusa.

The Divine Visitors

Only after committing himself to the goal of killing the Gorgon did Perseus truly realize the tremendous difficulty of the task. First, he did not know where to find the monster. Second, even if he could find her, he lacked a sword strong enough to penetrate her tough hide. And third, there was the problem of devising a way to fight her without having to look directly at her. Hoping to discover the whereabouts of the Gorgons, Perseus sailed to the Greek mainland and journeyed to Delphi, home

of the oracle of Apollo. The priestess was not very helpful, however. All she said was that he should seek out a land where people ate acorns instead of wheat (which suggested an area of forests rather than plains). So the young man traveled farther north, to another famous oracle—that of Zeus at Dodona. The priestess there did not know where the Gorgons lived either. But she did provide Perseus with a crucial piece of information. From now on, she told him, he would be under the special protection of some powerful gods.

Fortunately for Perseus, this protection became apparent almost immediately. He was riding his horse along a country road less than an hour after departing Dodona when he encountered an unusually handsome young man carrying a golden staff with little wings on it. The young man greeted Perseus warmly as if he knew him. And stopping his horse, Perseus asked if the two had met at some time in the past. The young man answered that a small demonstration seemed to be in order and suddenly rose into the air and flitted like a bird around Perseus's head.

It was then that Perseus recognized the young man as Hermes, the swift-footed messenger god and protector of travelers. Landing back on his feet, Hermes told the man that the task he had undertaken was both difficult and perilous, but not impossible. The god would show him where the Gorgons dwelled. However, to fight and defeat Medusa he would need some very special equipment, which only a group of young maidens—the Nymphs of the North—possessed. The problem was that the only ones who knew where the Nymphs lived were the grizzled old Graeae. Because they were the Gorgons' sisters, it was unlikely that they would agree to help Perseus, so he would have to devise a way to force the information from them. In the meantime, Hermes produced a magnificent sword seemingly out of thin air and handed it to Perseus. With it, the god said, the man would be able to cut through Medusa's thick hide.

Perseus still had one very important question: How would he be able to avoid the Gorgon's gaze and keep himself from becoming a pillar of stone, as had been the fate of so many men and women before him? The answer to this question did not come from Hermes, however; for,° at that moment, the startled Perseus looked up and beheld a radiant golden ball descending from the sky. Suddenly, the ball seemed to burst, revealing the goddess Athena, dressed in her splendid suit of armor. She greeted Perseus and then removed a shield of polished bronze from her chest. He should use this shield, she said, when he approached the Gorgon, for the simple reason that, though her image was lethal when viewed directly, her reflection was harmless. She explained that Hermes would take Perseus to the withered ones—the Graeae. They would tell him how he could find the Nymphs and acquire the rest of his equipment. After wishing the young hero good luck, the goddess became a radiant ball once more and ascended into the sky.

Six Monstrous Sisters Are Outwitted

Guided by Hermes, Perseus journeyed to the gray, dismal land where the Graeae lived. Eventually the god pointed to three figures huddled near the entrance to a large cave. At first glance, Perseus thought that the creatures resembled large birds, but on closer inspection he could see that they had human heads and hands, which were covered with wrinkles and age spots. The man and his divine companion hid behind a rock and watched the weird sisters closely. Each time one of them wanted to look at something, she took the eye out of her sister's forehead and placed it in an empty socket in her own forehead. In this manner, they swapped the eye back and forth every minute or so. A plan began to take shape in Perseus's head, and soon he knew what he had to do.

The young man suddenly stepped forward and revealed himself to the Graeae, who regarded him warily. What did the stranger want? one of them demanded.

Perseus answered that he sought the location of the Nymphs of the North. Recoiling in horror, the sisters wailed in unison, refused to give him this information, and ordered him to go away. Perseus had fully expected this reaction, of course, and now he put his plan into action. He moved abruptly to one side, then to the other, forcing the sisters to pass the eye hastily back and forth to keep track of him, and as

In this modern illustration, Perseus confronts the Graeae, the blind sisters of the Gorgons.

they did, he suddenly snatched the eye from one of their hands. If they wanted it back, he said, they must tell him how to find the Nymphs.

Needless to say, the Graeae, who had been stricken blind by the loss of their only eye, relented and gave Perseus the information he sought. Accompanied by the faithful Hermes, he followed their directions northward to the land of a happy people called the Hyperboreans. There, the travelers found the Nymphs of the North, who gave Perseus three gifts. The first was a pair of winged sandals similar to those Hermes wore. The second was a special sack that conformed in size to whatever one put into it. And the third gift was a cap that made its wearer invisible. At last, Perseus was ready to confront the monstrous Medusa.

In the words of the ancient Roman myth teller Ovid, Perseus, guided by Hermes, now flew "through unknown ways, thick-bearded forests, and tearing rocks and stones, until he found the Gorgons' home. And as he looked about from left to right, no matter where he turned, he saw both man and beast turned into stone, all creatures who had seen Medusa's face."[9] Finally, by their reflection in his shield, Perseus beheld the three Gorgons, who lay sleeping on a large rock. The man was startled when, without warning, Medusa awakened. Thanks to the keen senses of the writhing green serpents on her head, she could tell that danger was near; but because of her stalker's cap of invisibility, she could not see him. Being careful to look at her only by reflection, Perseus swooped down at her, his mighty sword raised to strike. Guided by Athena, who appeared on the scene at the crucial moment, the weapon sliced through Medusa's neck, severing her monstrous head from her equally repellent body. Skillfully, Perseus caught the head in his magic sack. At that moment, the other two Gorgons woke up, and seeing that their sister had been slain, they searched frantically for the killer. But Perseus was still invisible, so they could not find him.

Returning to the island of Seriphos, Perseus learned that his mother was being persecuted by King Polydectes. Having decided not to marry Hippodameia, Polydectes had resorted to threats to force Danae to marry him. Furious, Perseus flew to the palace. There, he removed the cap of invisibility and confronted the king and his supporters, who drew their swords and prepared to attack him. Reaching into the sack, Perseus pulled out the repulsive snake-haired head and held it up. Instantly, the king and his courtiers froze in their tracks, the light of

A nineteenth-century illustration depicts Perseus slaying Medusa and taking care to avoid looking directly at her severed head.

life faded from their eyes, and their bodies quickly calcified into motionless stone pillars. The eerie truth was that even in death the monster Medusa retained her petrifying power.

The Harpies and Old Phineus

Another group of female monsters was distantly related to the creatures Perseus outwitted, and like the Gorgons, these creatures, the Harpies, were hideous. Phorcys and Ceto, who had sired the Graeae and Gorgons, had a brother named Thaumas. He mated with Electra, daughter of the Titan named Oceanus, and among their offspring were the Harpies, flying creatures with sharp beaks and claws, women's faces, and a sickening stench. No one knows why Electra and Thaumas gave rise to such ugly and disgusting creatures. In any case, though, Zeus took advantage of their existence by sending them out to punish mortals with whom he was angry.

One of the most famous tales of the Harpies is the one that recalls their encounter with Jason and the Argonauts.

In this eighteenth-century engraving, the Argonauts rescue poor old Phineus from the Harpies, seen fleeing at upper right.

Jason and the Serpent

In addition to the Harpies, Jason and his Argonauts met up with several other monsters on their fateful journey to Colchis to retrieve the Golden Fleece. They battled a giant named Talos, and when they reached Colchis, Jason had to fight two fire-breathing bulls as well as the deadly serpent that guarded the tree that held the Fleece. In this excerpt from his epic poem the *Argonautica*, the third-century B.C. Greek writer Apollonius of Rhodes describes Jason's encounter with the serpent, in which a sorceress named Medea aids the hero.

The serpent, with his sharp unsleeping eyes, had seen them coming and now confronted them, stretching out his long neck and hissing terribly. . . . The monster in his sheath of horny scales rolled forward his interminable [seemingly endless] coils, like the eddies of black smoke that spring from smoldering logs and chase each other from below in endless convolutions [twists and turns]. But as he writhed, he saw the maiden take her stand, and heard her in her sweet voice invoking sleep . . . to charm him. . . . Jason, from behind, looked on in terror. But the giant snake, enchanted by her song, was soon relaxing the whole length of his spike-covered spine . . . like a dark and silent swell rolling across a sluggish sea. . . . Sleep fell on him. Stirring no more, he let his jaw sink to the ground. . . . Medea called to Jason, and he snatched the Golden Fleece from the oak.

The hero Jason and his men, members of the crew of a stout ship called the *Argo*, were on a mission to recover the Golden Fleece. This fabulous, priceless skin of a magical lamb was guarded by a dragon in the land of Colchis, located on the far shore of the Black Sea.

During their trip, the Argonauts beached their ship each evening since it was not large enough to hold many supplies and they had to search frequently for food. One evening they came ashore on the European coast of the Bosphorus (one of the two narrow channels that divide the Aegean and Black Seas). There, they found an old man named Phineus, who

was so starved and emaciated that all that was left of him was quite literally skin and bones. Jason asked the poor fellow what had happened to him. Phineus answered that Apollo had once granted him the gift of prophecy, but that Zeus did not like the idea of humans knowing what he was going to do next, so Zeus had inflicted a punishment on Phineus. Every time the man began to eat a meal, the Harpies, whom some people called Zeus's Hounds, swooped down and either stole his food or covered it with their vile stench, making it too disgusting for him to eat.

Jason and his men decided to help old Phineus. Two of the Argonauts, Zetes and

Calais, were the sons of Boreas, the North Wind. Thanks to their ancestry, they possessed the ability to fly through the air, which gave them the best chance in a fight against flying creatures like the Harpies. Jason and the others gathered up a huge amount of food and prepared a magnificent banquet for Phineus. Meanwhile, Zetes and Calais stood on either side of the old man, their swords drawn and ready in case the Harpies appeared. Sure enough, as told by the Greek writer Apollonius in his epic poem about the *Argo's* voyage,

> Phineus had scarcely lifted the first morsel [of food], when, with as little warning as a whirlwind or a lightning flash, the Harpies dropped from the clouds proclaiming their desire for food with raucous cries. [Before the warriors could react], the Harpies had devoured the whole meal and were on the wing once more, far out to sea. All they left behind was an intolerable stench. . . . Raising their swords, the two sons of the North Wind flew off in pursuit.[10]

Eventually Zetes and Calais caught up to the disgusting creatures. And the men would surely have cut them to pieces, but the goddess of the rainbow, Iris, intervened. Iris was a sister of the Harpies, and she sought to protect them. She told Zetes and Calais that they must not kill Zeus's Hounds. If they would spare the Harpies, she said, she would give them her word that the creatures would never go near old Phineus again. Iris did indeed keep her word, and thereafter Phineus was able to eat his fill without harassment. Jason and his men continued on their voyage to faraway Colchis, taking with them some valuable advice from Phineus about the potential dangers that lay ahead.

As in the cases of the Sphinx and the snake-haired Medusa, the Harpies were ultimately defeated by mortal men. And in this way the theme of a male triumph over a female threat was reenacted repeatedly in Greek myths. The message was fairly straightforward. Women who aspired to too many rights and too much power in society would be viewed in the same way as the monsters of myth—as dangers to be eliminated.

Ancient Persia: The Battle Between Good and Evil

I n ancient Greek mythology monsters were often capable of evil deeds; in Persian mythology, however, they were portrayed literally as the embodiments of evil. For example, every ancient Persian was familiar with the demon Azhi Dahaka, whom the Persian holy book the *Avesta* described as "the three-mouthed, the three-headed, the six-eyed creature who has a thousand senses, that most powerful, fiendish demon, baleful to the world."[11] The *Avesta*, which contains many of the original Persian myths about monsters and the heroes who opposed them, was the bible, so to speak, of the chief religion of the ancient Persians—Zoroastrianism. Its founder, Zoroaster

(also called Zarathustra), was a semimythical figure who possibly lived sometime between 1400 and 1000 B.C.

The exact origins of Zoroaster and his immediate followers are not known. What is certain is that by about 800 B.C. or so, groups of nomadic peoples whom modern scholars call Indo-Iranians had settled north of the Persian Gulf in what is now Iran. Two of these groups, the Medes and the Persians, became dominant. And after conquering the Medes in the sixth century B.C., the Persian prince Cyrus the Great established the Persian Empire, which within a generation stretched from the borders of India in the east to the Mediterranean coast in the west.

Iran's Early Inhabitants

The people that produced the rich Zoroastrian mythology of good versus evil originated somewhere in the steppes of central Asia. Periodic migrations of nomadic peoples southward from this region occurred throughout the second millennium B.C. Perhaps sometime between 1100 and 1000 B.C. (the exact date being much disputed by scholars) small groups identifying themselves as "Aryans" descended onto the mountainous plateau that rises north of the Persian Gulf. The name Iran, which later came to identify the region, is derived from the word Aryanam, meaning "Land of the Aryans." Surviving ancient annals reveal that by the mid-ninth century B.C. two Aryan peoples were well established in Iran. The Mada, whom we call the Medes, settled mainly in the northwestern portion of the plateau around the city of Ecbatana (modern Hamadan); and the Parsua, or Persians, eventually occupied the land of Fars, directly north of the gulf.

The Medes were the first of these two new Iranian peoples to gain military and political prominence in Near Eastern affairs. They were apparently strong enough by the mid-700s B.C. to pose at least a moderate threat to the Assyrians, then the leading power in Mesopotamia, the region lying to the west of Iran. Assyrian annals record two campaigns against the Medes, led by King Tiglath Pileser III (reigned 744–727) and King Sargon (721–705), respectively.

Assyrian carved wall reliefs from this era depict Median fortresses with high battlements equipped with notches through which defenders could hurl missile weapons at attackers. Reflecting their unpolished nomadic roots, the Medes themselves appear on these reliefs with short hair, short curled beards, and red headbands. They wore tunics, covered in winter by sheepskin coats, and high-laced boots for walking and fighting in deep snow. For weapons, they carried a long spear and a rectangular wicker shield. The Medes also employed archers on horseback, a military practice inherited from their ancestors, the nomads of the central Asian steppes.

Persian and Median noblemen walk together in this sculpture from a Persian palace.

A modern rendering of the ancient Persian prophet Zoroaster, also sometimes called Zarathustra, who lived between 1400 and 1000 B.C.

Cyrus's immediate successors were all devout followers of Zoroaster, and at some time during their reigns, the *Avesta* may have been written down for the first time. (Before this, its contents were passed along by oral means.) According to some stories, this version, which was set down in gold letters on an ox hide, was destroyed when the Greek conqueror Alexander the Great invaded Persia in the fourth century B.C. Over the course of the centuries, parts of the *Avesta* were committed to writing again. But these versions have not survived either. Fortunately, a version from the thirteenth or fourteenth century has survived; unfortu-

nately, though, it represents only a fraction of the original. Some of the gaps in Zoroastrian Persian mythology were filled in by an Islamic poet named Firdausi, who lived about A.D. 1000. He wrote a long poem, the *Shahnameh (Book of Kings)*, based on a number of the now lost Zoroastrian texts.

The monsters mentioned in these mythological sources most often take the form of evil demons (*div*) and dragons, or demons who were themselves dragons (although stories about witches, giant birds, and other evil creatures exist). Evil is certainly the operative term here. This is because the central core of the religion and mythology of ancient Persia consists of a nearly eternal battle between good and evil. According to Zoroaster, the forces of the truth (or order) naturally oppose the forces of the lie (or disorder). In this cosmic scheme, good and innocent people are the followers of the truth, the *ashavans*; whereas wicked or corrupt people are the followers of the lie, the *drugvans*. In the words of scholar John R. Hinnells of Manchester University,

> To the Zoroastrians, there can be no greater sin than to associate good with evil, that is, to suggest that the good world is the creation of the Evil Spirit. The opposite applies equally forcefully. There can be no greater sin than to associate God with evil. Good and evil are contrary realities, as are darkness and light, or life and

This painting of Persian horsemen charging an enemy army comes from a copy of Firdausi's Shahnameh *dated to the fourteenth century.*

death. . . . Good and evil cannot co-exist; they are mutually destructive. . . . The opposition of good and evil or God and the devil, to use Christian terms, is the basis of all Zoroastrian mythology, theology, and philosophy.[12]

The Prince of Darkness

This opposition between the forces of good and evil is the central theme of the myths surrounding the dreaded demon Azhi Dahaka. This hideous creature, who sometimes appeared as a dragon or a ser-

pent and at other times as the driving force of the storm clouds, was one of the leading *drugvans*. He was happiest when the world was in darkness and humanity was in misery. Azhi Dahaka grew angry, therefore, when he saw the human hero Takhmoruw fight and subjugate most of his fellow demons. Takhmoruw made himself king, brought peace and light to the world, encouraged industry and morality, and forced the demons, whom he had put in chains, to toil at the lowliest tasks. And eventually the goodly king passed along his throne and the better society he had created to his son, Yima (also known as Jamshid).

Unfortunately for humanity, but quite fortunately for Ahzi Dahaka, Yima made a fatal mistake as ruler. The king, who was a good and courageous man at heart, allowed his high position and tremendous power to go to his head and cloud his judgment. He became conceited and sought to overshadow Ahura Mazda, the great and kind god from whom all goodness emanated. According to the *Shahnameh,*

> One day when he was contemplating the throne of power, Yima deemed that he was peerless. He knew God, but displayed ingratitude and disobedience and turned away from God. Yima summoned all the high officials and told them: "The world is mine. . . . The royal throne has never seen a king like me, for I have decked the world with excellence and fashioned earth according to my will. . . . Who dares to say that there is any greater king than me? . . . You owe me sense, and life, and everything. Those who do not love me are followers of the Lie and the Evil One. So now you must hail me as the Maker of the world and worship me!"[13]

Yima soon learned the hard way that he had made an error of enormous scope, one that brought with it terrible consequences. As kings ruling with the grace of Ahura Mazda, he and his father had glowed with a special divine radiance (known as the *Khvarenanh,* or "Glory") sent by the high god. Only minutes after Yima turned away from God, however, the radiance disappeared. Moreover, the nobles and the people were disappointed and angry that he had come to fancy himself a god, and they deserted him.

Hearing what had happened, Ahzi Dahaka chortled with glee. The millions of scorpions, lizards, and other vile creatures that filled his huge demonic body danced and slithered, itching to be

A Persian king grapples with a demon in this relief sculpture found at the ancient Persian palace at Persepolis.

released onto the earth. Yima had grown weak, the demon reasoned, and his protector, the god Ahura Mazda, had abandoned him. Clearly, this seemed like Ahzi Dahaka's big chance to overthrow Yima, seize his throne, and free his fellow demons from their bondage. Bursting forth from his dark lair in the storm clouds, Ahzi Dahaka swooped down and headed straight for Yima's palace. Terrified at the sight of the gigantic dragonlike beast approaching, the king abandoned his throne and fled into hiding. The demon triumphantly entered the royal court, where the fearful nobles fell on their faces before him. The prince of darkness was now the king of the world, Ahzi Dahaka hissed at them, and they now had no choice but to do his bidding!

The Demon's Dream Becomes Reality

Indeed, Ahzi Dahaka lived up to his reputation as a prince of darkness. The sun was no longer seen, and a perpetual dim twilight descended on the earth. At the new king's order, the demons were released from their bondage and roamed far and

Contrasting Pairs in the Zoroastrian Universe

The repeated emphasis on good versus evil, light versus dark, and so forth in the Zoroastrian faith and its writings makes for a universe dominated by dual elements, or contrasting pairs. The following list of such pairs comes from a ninth-century A.D. Zoroastrian text called the *Book of Primal Creation* (quoted in editor Mary Boyce's *Textual Sources for the Study of Zoroastrianism*).

Falsehood and deceit are against Truthfulness; the sorcerer's spell against the holy words; excess and deficiency against right measure. Bad thought, word, and deed are against good thought, word and deed. . . . Aimless lust is against innate wisdom. . . . Idleness is against diligence; sloth [laziness] against needful sleep; vengefulness against peace; pain against pleasure; stench against fragrance; darkness against light . . . bitterness against sweetness. . . winter against summer; cold against heat . . . defilement [contamination] against cleanliness; pollution against purification; discontent against contentment. . . . Likewise among the physical creations, hell is against the sky; drought against water, impurity and noxious creatures [scorpions, lizards, etc.] against the earth; insects against plants. . . . The lion and the predatory wolf-species are against the dog and cattle, the toad against fishes. . . . Wicked apostates [nonbelievers] are against just men; the whore against women . . . the demon of destruction against long life.

The winged disk above these Persian sphinxes was the symbol of the great Persian god Ahura Mazda.

graces and attempt to regain the throne. For nearly a hundred years, Ahzi Dahaka had his demons and other henchmen search for Yima, who managed to stay hidden. Finally, however, someone recognized the former king, who was now a very old man, and he was captured. Thrilled to have his enemy in custody at last, Ahzi Dahaka ordered his executioners to saw Yima in half, from the top of his head straight downward. The demon-king reasoned that now nothing could stand in his way and that he would surely rule forever. And so it was written, "Ahzi Dahaka sat on the throne for a thousand years, obeyed by everyone on earth. All through these years, wise men were out of fashion, goodness was despised, the black arts thrived . . . and [for humans] disaster was ever-present."[14]

Ahzi Dahaka's prediction that he would rule forever proved overconfident, however. One night the demon had a dream in which he saw a mighty hero rise up and vanquish him. Fearful that the dream might come true, the king ordered his army of demons to keep on the lookout for any human who appeared out of the ordinary. Little did Ahzi Dahaka know that the young hero whom he dreaded, whose name was Thraetaona (also called Faridun), was already attempting to assemble the

wide, causing mischief and destruction at will. The people were oppressed and had no one to turn to for justice. Meanwhile, each day Ahzi Dahaka had two young men killed so that he could feed their brains to two red-eyed serpents that grew out of his chest. This sad, brutal state of affairs continued month after month, year after year, with no end in sight.

Ahzi Dahaka was pleased, of course, that his dream of holding absolute power over the earth had finally been achieved. Only one thing kept him from attaining true demonic happiness. This was the fact that Yima was still alive; as long as the former ruler lived, the chance existed that he might find some way back into God's good followers he needed to launch a rebellion. Luckily for Thraetaona, there was a group of nobles who were sick and tired of the demon's unjust reign. They were led by a man named Kaveh, whose eighteen sons had been killed and fed to the king's brain-eating serpents. Kaveh and his men joined Thraetaona and pledged to fight with him against the evil creature who occupied the throne.

When all of the preparations were made, Thraetaona led his army through deep forests and across fields and deserts until he came to the royal castle, which towered high into the clouds. The dragon-king Ahzi Dahaka saw that he would have to fight for the throne. Gathering his demon-soldiers, he rode out through the castle gates and met the rebels in battle. Many fell on both sides; eventually Ahzi

Time Affects Both Good and Evil

Opposing the various monstrous demons of Persian mythology is, of course, the ultimate god of goodness, wisdom, and knowledge—Ahura Mazda, "the Wise Lord." This tract from an old Zoroastrian Persian text (quoted in editor Mircea Eliade's *Essential Sacred Writings from Around the World*) tells how both this great god and his evil counterpart, the demon-monster Angra Mainyu (or Destructive Spirit), exist in time and how they, like mortal humans, are subject to the effects of time's passage.

By his clear vision, Ahura Mazda saw that the Destructive Spirit would never cease from aggression and that his aggression could only be made fruitless by the act of creation, and that creation could not move on except through Time. . . . [Therefore] he [Ahura Mazda] fashioned forth Time. And the reason was this, that the Destructive Spirit could not be made powerless unless he were brought to battle. . . . In his unrighteous creation, Angra Mainyu was without knowledge, without method. And the reason . . . is this, that when Angra Mainyu joined battle with Ahura Mazda the majestic wisdom, renown, perfection, and permanence of Ahura Mazda and the powerlessness, self-will, imperfection, and slowness in knowledge of the Destructive Spirit were made manifest when creation was created. . . . As it is said in the Religion [of the prophet Zoroaster], "Time is mightier than both creations—the creation of Ahura Mazda and that of the Destructive Spirit. Time understands all action and order (the law). Time understands more than those who understand. Time is better-informed than the well-informed; for through Time must the decision be made. By Time are houses overturned—doom is through Time—and things graven [made] shattered. From it [Time] no single mortal man escapes, not though he fly above, not though he dig a pit below and settle therein, not though he hide beneath a well of cold waters."

Dahaka and Thraetaona met face to face, and the hero exclaimed that the demon's day of judgment had finally come. At this, Thraetaona charged at the demon and struck him on the head with a mace (a heavy, spiked club). Ahzi Dahaka fell from his horse and lay bleeding on the ground. The young man had won, the demon reluctantly admitted, so he should go ahead and finish the job by killing Ahzi Dahaka while he was down and defenseless, since this was what the demon would do if the situation were reversed. But Thraetaona refused. If he killed a defenseless being, as Ahzi Dahaka had slain poor Yima, he would be no better than an evil demon. So the defeated Ahzi Dahaka would be allowed to live, but it would be in a place where he could no longer exercise any power or hurt anyone.

Thraetaona had his men bind the demon, and they carried it to Mount Demavend, which lay at the far edge of the earth. Tunneling deep inside the hillside, they threw Ahzi Dahaka into a pitch-black cave and then filled in the only shaft leading into it with solid rock. Having entombed this enemy of humanity, Thraetaona became king, drove away the demons, and brought light and happiness back to the earth. All seemed right in the world again. No one, of course, including Thraetaona, could foresee what lay far in the future; according to the sacred *Avesta*, some day the evil monster Ahzi Dahaka will rise from his rocky tomb and once more spread fear and havoc across the face of the earth.

This exquisite rendering from the Shahnameh *shows King Kai-Kaus, who made the ill-fated decision to invade the land of Mazinderan.*

The White Demon's Trickery

Although Thraetaona had imprisoned Ahzi Dahaka and had driven away the other demons, some of these hideous creatures still lurked in caves and other hiding places on the edges of the civilized world. Over the succeeding centuries, they occasionally rose up and preyed on unwary travelers who strayed too close to their putrid lairs. One of these monsters, Div-e-Sepid, the so-called White Demon, was especially ugly, mean, and formidable. Its lair was located on the border of the faraway land of Mazinderan, located on the shores of the

Caspian Sea. Any travelers attempting to reach Mazinderan from Persia, which lay at the center of the civilized world, quickly fell prey to the White Demon and its band of monstrous followers (who were large, hairy, and smelly).

One day the White Demon decided that ordinary travelers were not sufficient prey to satisfy its appetite. In an unusual display of boldness, it decided to lure the ruler of Persia, King Kai-Kaus, to its lair, where it planned to rob him of his royal jewels and other treasures. The demon sent one of its followers, disguised as a human musician, to the court. The phony musician urged Kai-Kaus to take some soldiers and conquer the land of Mazinderan. It was a beautiful land, the musician explained, and a place rich in natural resources. Yet it had no army to speak of, so it would be easy to subdue. The king's best course, the musician concluded, would be to take along enough royal treasures and valuables to set up a new court in Mazinderan.

The White Demon's trickery worked. Though King Kai-Kaus did not normally take military advice from a mere musician, the man's words stuck in his mind. And after giving the matter much thought, the king decided to take the musician's advice and lead an expedition against the faraway and little-known land of Mazinderan.

Kai-Kaus was in the midst of his preparations when one of Persia's most respected heroes and senior statesmen, Zal, asked for an audience. Zal told the king that the new venture would be a serious mistake and begged him to reconsider. According to Zal, the border regions of Mazinderan were too dangerous because they were infested with demons and other monsters, the followers of the powerful White Demon. But no matter how much the older man pleaded with the king to reconsider, Kai-Kaus refused to change his plans. Zal worried too much, he said. The king added that he had heard that most of the demons were dead and that the few remaining ones were old and weak. And surely they would not dare to attack the king of Persia and his soldiers.

But Zal had good reason to be worried when he watched the expedition leave the capital and disappear over the horizon. The king was wrong to think that the demons were few in number and weak, as he learned, to his horror, when they attacked him and his forces. As told by noted mythologist Norma L. Goodrich, as Kai-Kaus approached the border of Mazinderan,

all of a sudden the sun began to be swallowed up! A great stillness fell over all the earth, and an increasing blackness. As it grew darker and darker, a huge storm gathered. . . . Terrified, the Persians listened as the sky inhaled. There was a moment of silence. Then the storm burst. In an explosive onslaught it blew across the flat tableland where the Persians huddled unprotected. . . . Arrows fell among the warriors from the bows of the white demons. The pack

The Simurgh, the magical bird that raised the hero Zal, is the subject of this Persian painting dating from about A.D. 1295.

animals trampled madly over the fallen warriors. . . . Kai-Kaus and his soldiers became completely blind. They could not even see the face of the White Demon when it appeared leering and ghostly white at the horizon's edge. They surrendered quietly to his 12,000 demons, who ripped off their jeweled collars and rings and tore their weapons from their sides.[15]

The Coming of Rustam

A few days later the news reached the Persian royal court that the king and his surviving soldiers had been captured and were being held prisoner in a cave by the White Demon. Zal was not surprised. He realized that he himself was too old and frail to be of any help, but he was confident that Persia's greatest hero, his son Rustam, could defeat the forces of evil and rescue the king. The other Persian nobles agreed that Rustam was by far the best man for the job.

Rustam's singular origins go a long way to explain the faith everyone had in his abilities. Long before Rustam was born, when Zal himself was an infant, Zal's father, a Persian noble, abandoned him on a hillside. The child would surely have died had it not been for the Simurgh, a large, powerful, and magical bird that took Zal in and raised him as its own offspring. Years passed and Zal's father, who had heard that his son was alive, had a change of heart. The kind and very wise Simurgh had foreseen such a development and now advised Zal to go and live with his human father; ultimately, the Simurgh said, a human belonged with his own kind. However, the great bird told Zal that he would always watch over him. According to the *Shahnameh,* the Simurgh gave Zal one of its feathers and said,

> Henceforth, if any men shall hurt you, or say bad things about you [or you encounter trouble of any kind], then burn this feather and behold my might [as I will then instantly appear at your side and help you], for I have cherished you beneath my plumes and brought you up among my little ones.[16]

Zal did as the Simurgh instructed. He went to live in his father's large house, and he soon met and married a beautiful princess named Rudabeh. She became pregnant, and when she was about to give birth, her labor pains proved far worse than a normal child would have caused. Zal was so worried that he burned the feather the Simurgh had given him. And sure enough, the great bird appeared, as if out of nowhere. Zal should not worry, the Simurgh said. Rudabeh's pains were great because the child that was about to be born was himself great. He would have the

height of a cypress tree, the strength of an elephant, and become the mightiest hero Persia had ever known. But care should be taken to make sure he was delivered by Caesarian section (that is, through an incision in the lower abdomen), or else the mother would not survive.

As usual, the Simurgh's words proved prophetic. The child, whom Zal and Rudabeh named Rustam, was truly extraordinary. When he was only a year old, he had the stature and strength of a normal ten-year-old. And by the time he was a young man, he could easily bring down a full-grown elephant with a single swing of his mace. Rustam searched long and hard for a horse that could match his own strength and courage. At last he found a magnificent steed and named it Rakhsh. Together, the two had various adventures, slew some fierce and dangerous animals, and faced down and vanquished several of the enemies of the Persian king.

Rustam the Monster Killer

Rustam's most important and dangerous test yet, however, was the one his father now proposed—to hurry across the mountains and deserts, defeat the White Demon and its monstrous followers, and release the king and his soldiers. The young man vowed that he would leave immediately and that he would not return until he had fully accomplished these goals. Gathering his weapons, he mounted Rakhsh and rode off in the direction of Mazinderan.

The journey turned out to be long and dangerous. But after many days Rustam and Rakhsh finally reached the cave where King Kai-Kaus and his soldiers were imprisoned. A hideous monster named Arzhang, which guarded the entrance, immediately rushed forward and attacked the intruders. But Rustam and his steed were so quick and nimble that they managed to sidestep the creature; and as it rushed by them, Rustam grabbed its head and tore it right off of its

In an illustration from a sixteenth-century version of the Shahnameh, *the hero Rustam is born via Caesarian section while several courtiers look on.*

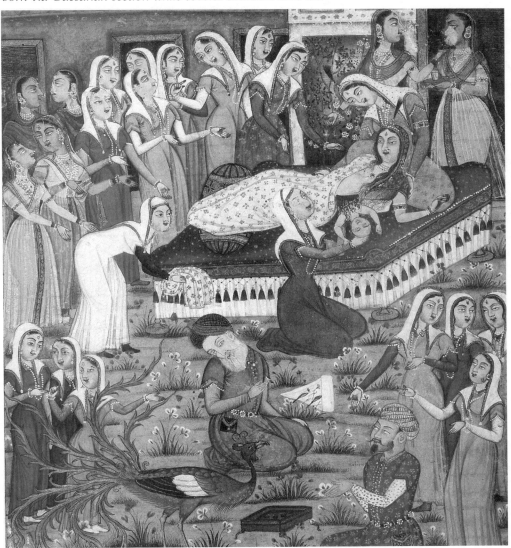

A late medieval Islamic illustration shows the mighty hero Rustam killing the White Demon.

body, which fell, bleeding, into the dust. The hero then tossed the gore-covered trophy into the camp the demons had erected nearby. When the demons saw the head, they panicked and ran away screaming. Rushing inside the cave, Rustam found that the king was alive but was still blind from the intensity of the White Demon's initial attack. Rustam had to bring back some of the White Demon's blood, Kai-Kaus told him, for only by sprinkling the blood on the king's eyes would his sight be restored.

Rustam leaped onto Rakhsh and galloped away toward the White Demon's lair. Reaching it, the young man issued a challenge, calling on the creature to come out and face him. The White Demon soon appeared, and after hurling several insults and threats, it picked up a huge stone and threw it at the man. But Rustam easily dodged the missile and himself went on the attack. First he sliced off one of the monster's feet, and then one of its hands. Next he swung his mighty mace, which smashed the creature's knees, crippling it. Finally, Rustam plunged his sword into the demon's heart, killing it. The man removed the White Demon's liver, mounted Rakhsh, and rode back to the king, whose sight was restored by blood that dripped out of the organ. All of Persia rejoiced when the king was restored to his throne; and both the king and the people expressed their heartfelt thanks to Rustam for ridding the world of some its most formidable monsters.

Both Azhi Dahaka and the White Demon had been defeated by human heroes. But in the eyes of ancient Persians, and in the core of their Zoroastrian beliefs, these heroes were more than just brave and stout monster killers. More importantly, they represented the forces of good, in the form of the truth, which must oppose evil, the guiding force behind the lie, at all costs. And it was seen as a battle destined to go on perhaps forever.

Ancient India: Demonic Enemies of Gods and Humans

In the myths of ancient India, some monsters actually acquired enough power to contend at times on an equal footing with the gods. In fact, some of these monsters were originally gods themselves. To appreciate how this came to be, first consider that the monsters of Indian mythology, like those of Persian (Iranian) mythology, most often take the form of evil demons. One reason for this similarity of beliefs is that both peoples had common roots. Iran was settled by migrating Aryans who came from central Asia; another branch of the Aryans pushed into northern India, perhaps beginning their migration in about 1800 B.C. (Over the course of the next few centuries, some of these invaders moved steadily southward and eventually crossed to the island of Sri Lanka, located off of India's southeastern coast.) The early Aryans, a warlike people who knew neither cities nor the art of writing, subjugated the indigenous Indians, whom modern scholars generally refer to as Dravidians.

In time, however, the Aryan and Dravidian cultures mingled and exchanged ideas and beliefs. In fact, the Hindu faith, with its attending collection of gods and myths, is a product of this mixing. Many of these characters and stories were recorded in writing in the sacred *Vedas*, a series of compilations of hymns completed perhaps between 1000 and 900 B.C. (Gods personified in the *Vedas* are said to be "Vedic.") Thereafter, Indian religion continued to evolve, and in the process, still other mythical characters and their stories were incorporated into Hindu beliefs. Rather than being incorporated into the older texts, these new stories were written down separately. And most of these newer texts, including the great *Ramayana* (written down between 200 B.C. and A.D. 200), tended to retain many of the older gods and demons, although they sometimes gave them different names and altered roles or attributes.

One important outcome of this often complex process of religious evolution is that some of the characters who were originally gods later came to be viewed as demon-monsters, the *asuras*. Myths naturally developed to explain this demotion. Usually, the myths ran, as gods they erred somehow and were driven from the heavens by the *devas* (the unerring gods) and into the infernal (underground) regions or beneath the sea. Yet this loss of status did not diminish the power of the *asuras*. Indeed, they became potent, ongoing threats to the gods and to humanity. "One

This painting, dating from about A.D. 1275, shows a battle between the goddess Durga, one of the devas, *and one of the monstrous* asuras.

The great Indian hero Rama and two companions are depicted in this illustration from an eighteenth-century version of the Ramayana.

of the unusual features of Indian mythology," writes noted expert Veronica Ions,

> is that gods and demons are of equal strength and constantly fight for dominion of the three worlds [the heavens, the earth, and the air between]. In Hindu mythology . . . the gods are not always able to keep control of heaven. They owed their appearance of strength at first to their monopoly of soma [a drink that increased their strength] and in general to the sacrifices offered to them by humans. The demons were ever-watchful for an oppor-
> tunity to snatch the soma, but the gods, being already fortified with it, could fight them off. Alternatively, the gods used ruses to keep it from them. The demons, for their part, and especially in later times, could acquire great power and force concessions out of the great gods. . . . But again, the gods usually outwitted them, by sheer trickery . . . or by secret prayers and the like.[17]

The Deadly Cloud Demon

One of the most famous such Indian myths about a god outwitting and defeating a monster involves the dreaded demon Vritra. This demonic creature dwelled inside of clouds, where it sucked up moisture, keeping it from falling as rain. Vritra, therefore, brought drought, which reduced fields to dust bowls, causing many people to suffer hunger or even to die of starvation.

The nemesis of this much-feared *asura* was the mighty Indra, the most dynamic and revered of the early Vedic gods. According to legend, Indra was born at about the time that Vritra started the most devastating drought ever. Indra's mother, Prithivi (the earth), and father, Dyaus (the sky), listened with great distress day after day to the worried and eventually anguished cries of humans. But since Vritra was as strong as or stronger than any of the gods, none of these deities wanted to risk a fight with the demon.

As the human pleadings continued unabated, one day Prithivi felt a pain in her abdomen and realized that she was about to give birth. Soon, out of her side came Indra, whose entrance into the world was so forceful that the heavens, ground, and mountains all shook. The existing gods, including Prithivi and Dyaus, were afraid because it seemed to them that this highly unusual infant might somehow upset the divine order or cause them other sorts of problems.

Indra immediately showed that the anxiety many of the gods felt was well founded. Shortly after his auspicious birth, for instance, he developed an enormous and seemingly insatiable appetite for food and drink. He ate two or three water buffalo at a single sitting (and as many as twenty or thirty at a time later on as an adult), and he guzzled as much soma as he could get his hands on. Soma, or "pressed juice," the gods' favorite drink, was an intoxicating liquid that granted great strength, among other benefits. The plant from which it was derived, writes scholar A. Berriedale Keith,

> yielded, when its roots were pressed, a juice which after careful straining was offered, pure or mixed with milk, to the gods. . . .

A magnificent bronze figurine of the god Indra, dating from about the thirteenth century.

A Hymn to Indra

This hymn, from the collection of early Indian sacred writings known as the *Rig Veda* (as translated by A. A. Macdonell in his *A Vedic Reader for Students*), describes and pays homage to the prominent Vedic god Indra, who slew the monster Vritra.

The chief wise god who as soon as born surpassed the gods in power;
Before whose vehemence the two worlds trembled by reason of the greatness of his valor: He,
*   O men, is Indra.*
Who made firm the quaking earth, who set at rest the agitated mountains . . .
Who having slain the serpent [Vritra] released the seven streams . . .
Who between two rocks has produced fire, victor in battles: He, O men, is Indra. . . .
The terrible one of whom they ask, "Where is he?", of whom they also say, "He is not."
He diminishes the possessions of the foe like the stakes of gamblers.
Believe in him: He, O men, is Indra. . . .
Even Heaven and Earth bow down before him; before his vehemence even the mountains
*   are afraid.*
Who is known as the Soma-drinker, holding the [thunder]bolt in his arm, who holds the bolt
*   in his hand: He, O men, is Indra.*

The color was brown or ruddy. . . . Besides milk, sour milk and barley water were commonly added. . . . It was a plant that conferred powers beyond the natural, and thus soma was the drink of immortality. . . . The gods loved it.[18]

Of all of the gods, it was Indra who most loved soma. And to get it in the quantities he desired, he stole some from his father and fought with some of the other gods.

In addition to his prodigious appetite, Indra early on showed unusual physical prowess. He had enormous strength, in part because he drank so much soma; he easily wielded his father's thunderbolt in his right hand; and he quickly learned to ride through the sky in a magnificent golden chariot drawn by two huge horses.

A Battle in the Clouds

The young Indra also possessed extraordinary courage and compassion. As his parents had, he heard the humans pleading for someone to come to their aid against the demon Vritra. But unlike his parents, he was not afraid to tangle with the demon. Indra told his mother that someone had to stop the monster that was depriving the world of the water it needed. She agreed but pointed out that Vritra was very strong and also very savage. It would take a god of monumental strength and bravery to face it in battle, she said. Hearing this, Indra grasped his thunderbolt and jumped into his chariot. He would do it, he declared with conviction—he would slay the demon and release the water it had been accumulating within its gigantic body. Before Prithivi could object, the stalwart young god charged away across the sky.

When people in various cities, villages, and farms saw Indra riding overhead, they became optimistic. They cheered him and shouted encouragement, hoping he would succeed in killing Vritra and ending the devastating drought. Everywhere people prayed and sang hymns, and priests performed sacrifices in Indra's honor. At the same time, a large number of human warriors donned their armor and went out to offer Indra their assistance. He shouted to them to follow him and urged them to help him destroy the demon's stone-walled fortresses, of which there were ninety-nine. And indeed, Indra and his followers proceeded to storm and wreck all of the fortresses in only a few days.

At this point mighty Indra was almost ready to confront the monster itself. All that remained to prepare the young god for the battle was for him to take a healthy drink of soma to fortify himself. Though it took him several days, he finally found three whole lakes filled with the coveted liquid and quickly drank them dry. Sec-

onds later a huge burst of energy pulsed through Indra's body, and he raced straight up to the cloud in which Vritra had recently taken up residence. Who dared to trespass on the property of the great Vritra? the monster demanded in a loud, deep-throated voice. Indra saw that the demon, which had serpentlike scales and red, piercing eyes, was a dozen times his size; but even in the face of so formidable a foe, the god remained unafraid. It was the son of Prithivi and Dyaus who had come, Indra said. He told the demon that he had come to rid the world of its disgusting carcass. At this, Vritra smiled obscenely, revealing a mouthful of sharklike teeth, and bragged that it could not be killed. The demon arrogantly dismissed the young god, calling him a puny, pathetic being with delusions of grandeur.

Instead, however, it was Vritra's own delusions of grandeur that were about to end. Leaping high over the surprised demon's head, the god hurled his thunderbolt into its upper back; a great shiver and spasm ran through the creature's body as the weapon pierced and smashed its heart, liver, and other vital organs. Vritra let out one last scream of defiance mixed with shock and horror and exploded, unleashing giant torrents of water that poured earthward and filled the streams and lakes. Indra then heard a strange sound. Listening intently, he suddenly realized that it was the din of a million human voices from below, all raised in a prayer of thanksgiving. And he was mightily pleased.

The Cannibal-Demon's Last Victim

Though the world rejoiced at Indra's defeat of Vritra, the forces of evil were by no means eliminated. Many more *asuras* and other kinds of monsters still roamed freely in various sections of the world, and from time to time they came into contact with and threatened human settlements. Vritra had consumed mainly water, but some of the other *asuras* were cannibals who feasted on human flesh. One of these cannibalistic demons was Baka, who stood some twenty feet tall and had nasty

Indra, brandishing daggers, rides toward his battle with the demon Vritra, in an Indian work created in the early nineteenth century.

red stains on his lips, chin, and chest from the blood that splattered out each day while he was eating.

Baka's usual practice was to attack a town, devour all of its inhabitants, and then move on to the next town. But in time the monster came to realize that this was an unwise practice; once the population of a town was eliminated, it could never again be a potential source of food. Furthermore, Baka and the other cannibal-demons would eventually eat all of the humans in the world and be left without their favorite food. It made more sense, Baka told one of his fellow demons, to settle down and live near a prosperous village. There, a demon could eat the humans a few at a time. Meanwhile, those the demon did not eat would continue having children, thereby replenishing their numbers from one generation to another and providing a constant and secure food supply.

Baka put this nefarious policy into practice. He journeyed through India until he found a large, comfortable cave located near three prosperous villages. Demanding that the leaders of the villages meet with him, Baka told them that he had taken up permanent residence in the area and that if they wanted to escape complete annihilation, they must provide

A statue of Bhima, son of Vayu, god of the winds. Bhima defeated the cannibal demon, Baka.

him with tribute—that is, payment acknowledging submission. They were to give him two cartloads of vegetables and one human each day to satisfy his appetite; if they refused, he would eat everyone in their villages, which would thereafter cease to exist.

Reasoning that they had no other choice, the villagers gave in to the monster's demands. Each day they loaded up two carts with vegetables and made the heart-rending choice of choosing one of their number to become Baka's victim. This ritual went on for several months, until one of India's greatest heroes heard about what was happening. He was Bhima, son of the wind god, Vayu. Arriving on the scene, Bhima told the village elders to send him as the demon's next victim. He had killed several *asuras* in battle, he said, and he promised that he would eliminate this menace and restore the peace and security the villagers had once enjoyed.

The next day Bhima disguised himself as a simple villager and went to the designated spot in the forest where Baka always collected his tribute. There, while waiting for the demon to show up, Bhima grew hungry and decided to eat some of the vegetables that constituted part of the villagers' daily offering. And before long, Bhima, who was known as much for his huge appetite as for his courage and skill as a warrior, had polished off both cartloads of produce.

Suddenly, an angry voice demanded to know where the vegetables had gone. Bhima whirled around to see the demon approaching, its hideous mouth dripping saliva in anticipation of its meal. The man matter-of-factly informed Baka that he had eaten the vegetables and then warned the demon to go away or else suffer dire consequences. This made Baka's eyes go wide with surprise, for no human had ever dared to speak to him so boldly. Enraged, the demon strode toward Bhima, vowing to eat him alive for his insolence.

But the overconfident Baka did not anticipate the strength and speed of his opponent. As the demon tried to pounce on him, Bhima easily sidestepped him, grabbed him by the hair, and smashed his face into a tree trunk, knocking out all of his teeth. The startled monster screamed, and blood poured from his mouth. Then he stooped down to retrieve his teeth, which turned out to be a fatal mistake, for seeing the opportunity to strike, Bhima swung his trusty club. With a loud crack, the demon's skull shattered, his brains splattered in all directions, and his huge, lifeless body collapsed into the dirt.

On hearing of the hero's victory, the villagers rejoiced. That victory had an additional benefit for the people of India because, fearing that Bhima would kill them too, several of Baka's fellow demons decided to stop preying on humans and switched to eating animals.

King of the *Rakshasas*

Thanks to the efforts of heroes like Bhima, a good many of the deadly *asuras* were eliminated as enemies of the gods and humans (although some of them remained menaces). There was another class of demons, however, that was just as frightening, deadly, and dangerous, if not more so. These were the *rakshasas*. As described by Ions, they

> are of grotesque appearance, many of them gorilla-like and hideous to behold. . . . But they often adopt disguises to hide their monstrosity—especially their womenfolk, who sometimes

succeed in undermining the defenses of mortal men by bewitching them. . . . Without disguises, however, they present a great variety of deformity. Some are dwarfs, others like beanstalks; some fat, others emaciated; some have over-long arms; some only one eye, or only one ear; some have monstrous bellies; some have crooked legs, some one leg, some three and four; some have serpents' heads, others have donkeys', horses', or elephants' heads. Just as their appearance varies, so do their functions. There are the . . . darbas, who haunt cemeteries and eat the bodies of the dead. There are the panis, aerial [flying] demons who inspire foolish actions and encourage slander and disbelief. . . . There are the grahas, evil spirits who often cluster about the god of war, Karttikeya, and who possess people's souls and make them insane. Finally, there are the demons who specialize in attacking holy men.[19]

The most frightening and evil of the rakshasas was their king, Ravana. He committed all manner of evil acts, but he especially relished breaking every law and seducing and/or raping every woman he could. He was the largest of the demons, standing hundreds of feet tall, and he had ten heads, twenty arms, and a huge mouth filled with sharp teeth. Ravana was also extremely strong. It was said that he could snap off entire mountaintops and toss

A group of rakshasas, *perhaps the most evil of the demons, terrorize some women in this ancient Indian painting done on the ceiling of a palace.*

The Great Battle Against Ravana Begins

Here is the opening of the great battle between the forces of good (led by Rama) and evil (led by Ravana) before the city of Lanka, from the *Ramayana* (as told in English prose by Elizabeth Seeger).

At Rama's command, the monkeys, in hundreds and thousands, rushed upon the mountain that upheld Lanka and began to scale its heights, roaring like thunderclouds. They tore down the outposts and reached the foot of the walls. Then Ravana ordered his troops to attack, and they poured out of the gates like the winds that will sweep the earth at doomsday. With the banging of kettledrums, the blare of trumpets and conch

The forces of Rama and Ravana begin to fight in this nineteeth-century painting.

shells, they came forth in chariots and on elephants and horses, clad in mail and armed with every sort of weapon. An appalling battle began between them, the monkeys yelling, "Victory to Rama and Sugriva!", the demons shouting, "Glory to Ravana!" Although the demons were better armed, they were surprised and confused by the attacks of the monkeys, who could smash a chariot and kill its horses with one sweep of the huge branches they carried, or with their great rocks. Often they avoided the arrows and the lances of the foe by leaping upon the demons and crushing them in their powerful arms, biting them, or scratching their eyes out. . . . Rama and Lakshmana sent forth clouds of arrows from their bows, destroying the arrows of the enemy bowmen and slaying numberless soldiers. At the end of the first day, apes and demons, horses and elephants lay dead upon the field among broken chariots, swords, shields, and fallen banners. The monkeys, trusting in Rama and Lakshmana, were weary but triumphant, while the demons longed for the coming of the night that would put an end to the battle.

them into the ocean, stirring up huge waves that sank fishing boats and devastated human coastal villages.

During his long career of wickedness, Ravana tangled on a number of occasions with gods and heroes, including the storm god, Indra, and the great Vishnu, the god who preserved the stability of the universe (hence his nickname—"the Preserver"). None of these opponents had managed to kill Ravana, although his enormous body was covered with the scars sustained in these inconclusive battles. As Ravana continued to perpetrate outrages against the gods and humanity, his enemies longed for the day when a champion of goodness would finally succeed in slaying him.

A Female Demon Seeks Revenge

The immediate events leading up to that fateful day began when Vishnu came down to earth and, as was his practice each time he saw the forces of evil growing too strong, took human form. This was the seventh time Vishnu had taken such mortal form. And this particular human incarnation of the god, called an avatar, went by the name of Rama and was destined to become one of the greatest of all human heroes. Rama was born the son and heir to a powerful king named Dasaratha; after the child grew to young manhood, he married Sita, the beautiful daughter of Janaka, the ruler of a neighboring kingdom.

One day Rama and his half brother, Lakshmana, were hunting in the forest when they encountered a giantess, whom they recognized as the *rakshasa* Surpanakha, the evil sister of Ravana. Wanting to avoid trouble, the two men tried to steer clear of the demon. But Rama was so unbelievably handsome that the giantess fell madly in love with him at first sight and pursued him through the forest. Rama told her that she was wasting her energy, that he was married already to a lovely woman named Sita. However, perhaps his noble half brother, Lakshmana—the man standing beside him—might be interested in her advances because he presently had no wife. The giantess, who seemed to think this idea was acceptable, turned to Lakshmana and smiled coyly. But Lakshmana was thoroughly repulsed by her and rejected her.

At this, Surpanakha became enraged and vowed that she would exact revenge against the men who had spurned her. She endeavored to hurt them by attacking Sita. The demon tried to swallow the young woman but failed, and Lakshmana retaliated by cutting off Surpanakha's nose, ears, and breasts. Bleeding and screaming in pain and blind rage, the giantess rushed to the demon Khara, who, like Ravana, was her brother, and told him what had happened. She called on him to avenge her humiliation by killing Rama and his half brother. Indeed, she cried out that Sita should also be killed, as well as all of the offenders' loved ones and servants! Heeding this call, Khara quickly gathered up a host of several thousand *rakshasas* and led the creatures against

Rama. According to Elizabeth Seeger's telling of the *Ramayana,*

> Rama put on his coat of golden mail [scaled armor]. He strung his bow and . . . went out to meet the host, which looked like a mass of dark clouds at sunrise, while he was the sun that would dispel them all. The demons hurled their arrows and spears at him, and he called upon the divine weapons given him by [a wise man] when he was a boy. With one of these, he turned aside the demons' shafts and with another he sent forth not one but a hun- dred arrows at once that flew like serpents through the air, each seeking out its foe and piercing its heart. The demons shrieked and fell, like dry wood consumed by fire. Again and again Rama bent his bow like a sickle, sending forth the deadly arrows that seemed to darken the sun. He too was wounded, but he stood as calm as a bull under a downpour of rain. Hundreds of the fiends were slain upon the field among their fallen banners, their shields and bright swords, their helmets and ornaments. The rest fled in terror.[20]

The monkey general Hanuman tells Sita that Rama and his army are approaching to rescue her from the clutches of the evil Ravana.

When the news came of Rama's defeat of the demon army, Surpanakha was angrier than ever. This time she appealed directly to her older brother, the king of the *rakshasas*, Ravana. In his usual selfish way, he was less interested in avenging his sister's mutilation and more interested in what he could gain by helping her—namely, possession of the beautiful Sita. He disguised himself as a holy man and went to the forest where Sita liked to take her daily walk. Eventually, when he felt the time was right, he made his move, telling her (according to the *Ramayana*),

> I am Ravana, king of the demons, O Sita, before whom gods and men tremble. . . . Beyond the sea, on the summit of a mountain, stands my splendid city, Lanka, filled with every delight. O beautiful one, come and live with me there as my chief queen and forget the lot of mortal women. Think no more of Rama, who is but human and whose end is near. I, the lord of all demons, have come to you, pierced by the shafts of love; therefore yield to me, fair princess![21]

The Power of Goodness

Sita, however, was not swayed by the monster's advances and flatly rejected them. In response, Ravana revealed to her his true and quite hideous form and promptly kidnapped her and dragged her

to his fortified city of Lanka. Rama and Lakshmana were understandably upset when they heard about Sita's abduction. Rama immediately raised an army and then made an alliance with the king of the monkeys, Sugriva, whose own vast army of monkeys and bears joined Rama's troops.

As the great assembly marched toward Lanka, Rama approached the leading monkey general, Hanuman. Because he was a son of the wind god, Vayu, Hanuman had the ability to fly, so Rama sent him ahead to tell Sita that help was on the way. Arriving at Ravana's palace a few hours later, Hanuman told Sita to take heart, for her noble lord, Rama, was approaching even now with a vast army and soon would rescue her. When the monkey was about to leave, some of the *rakshasas* guarding Sita caught him and brought him before Ravana. The demon-king ordered his henchmen to set fire to Hanuman's tail. But this order backfired on Ravana, for the monkey managed to escape and, with his tail still ablaze, went running through the city, igniting fires everywhere.

By this time, Rama and his army were approaching Lanka. Wasting no time, the rescuers attacked the already burning city. And in response, Ravana unleashed his own army of demons. In the great and bloody battle that ensued, Ravana's hideous son, Indrajit, made his way through the ranks, sought out Rama and Lakshmana, and severely wounded both

The *Ramayana*

In this excerpt from an essay on Hindu beliefs (published in *Eerdmans' Handbook to the World's Religions*), noted religious scholar Raymond Hammer describes the importance to Indian society and thought of the great epic tale the *Ramayana*, which tells how the monster Ravana kidnapped Sita and then met his match in her husband, the hero Rama.

The basic thesis of . . . the Ramayana *(which has 24,000 couplets) . . . is that history is divided into cycles. At the beginning, righteousness and order (dharma) marks the world. But then, through four ages, standards deteriorate until the gods decide to destroy the world and fashion it afresh. The poem indicates the need to discover meaning and purpose, even during the period of disorder. The* Ramayana *is placed within the second age, when order, though under attack, is still largely intact. It is the story of intrigue, in which Rama is ousted from the throne and his faithful wife Sita abducted [by the demon Ravana] and taken off to Sri Lanka. . . . Rama is the personification of righteousness and is looked upon as one of the ten incarnations (avatars) of Vishnu. The notion grew up that the gods send one avatar for each age. (This same notion of a series of ages . . . and the appearance of a savior-figure in each age is also present in Buddhist thought.) In popular Hinduism, the Rama story is not only heard from earliest childhood, but becomes the basis for everyday life. Rama will be invoked at the start of any undertaking and thanked on its successful completion. His exploits become an example to follow and an encouragement to upright behavior. His name will be used to console the aged and chanted by the assembled mourners as the bodies of the dead are taken away for cremation. Sita, too, becomes the model of the faithful wife who is so identified with her husband that, at one time, she would even ascend the funeral pyre and be cremated with him. Sita is praised for the virtues of piety, loyalty, and unassuming courtesy.*

of them. Seeing this, Hanuman (who had by this time extinguished his burning tail) again proved his worth. The monkey general swiftly flew to the towering Himalayan Mountains in northern India and retrieved a magical herb that, it was said, could heal any wound instantly. Hurrying back to the battle, Hanuman applied the herb to Rama's and Laksh- mana's wounds, which indeed disappeared in seconds, returning the heroes to their full strength.

Most of the leading *rakshasas* were eventually killed, and the conflict was transformed into a mighty single combat between the heroic Rama and the demonic Ravana. "There followed a struggle as had never been seen on earth, when those two warriors tried to kill each other," the *Ramayana* recalls.

Both were skilled archers, both knew all the science of warfare, both had weapons made by the high gods, and neither had ever known defeat. Each sent forth a cloud of arrows as they circled about each other, each had impenetrable armor and stood unwounded. . . . Then, as he

The armies of Rama and Ravana battle furiously in this miniature painting dating from the sixteenth century and on display in New Delhi, India.

fought, Rama taunted his foe. "What a hero you are, O wicked wretch, to carry off a woman. . . . Today your head . . . shall roll in the dust, and vultures will drink the blood that flows from your wounds!" He was so angry that his friends feared to look upon his face, and even Ravana was dismayed. Rama's courage and strength seemed to be redoubled by his rage, and he poured such a rain of arrows on his foe that Ravana's heart fainted within him and he dropped his bow and sank down on the bench of his chariot.[22]

Finally, Rama shot Ravana with the strongest arrow he possessed; the deadly projectile pierced the demon's body, damaging his vital organs.

Lying in the dust, bleeding and dying, Ravana saw Rama standing triumphantly above him. With a sudden revelation, the demon-king realized that his opponent was not a mere mortal man but rather a powerful god. Rama confirmed that this was indeed the case. The once-fearsome Ravana then took his last feeble breath, and his body froze in the stillness of death.

Afterward, some of those present questioned whether the slain demon-king should receive a proper funeral since they did not want to honor his memory in any way. But that attitude was wrong, Rama told them. Though Ravana had been an evil monster who had done much harm, Rama said, he had also been a skilled warrior. Anyway, he was dead now, so he was no longer anyone's enemy. Later that day, thanks to the wise and generous Rama/Vishnu, the demon Ravana received a full funeral, showing how the power of goodness endeavors to redeem even the most wicked beings in existence.

Perhaps there was another, less obvious motive underlying Rama/Vishnu's respectful treatment of the fallen demon. He realized that many of the evil monsters had once been gods themselves, divine personages who had fallen from grace for one reason or another. To lose the force of goodness and be condemned to spend the rest of one's days performing evil deeds was a serious and sad demotion in status. And for that reason, to at least some degree, these beings deserved to be pitied.

Ancient Africa: Shape-Shifters, Imps, and River Monsters

Africa, with its wide diversity of peoples and cultures, is home to an enormously varied body of mythical beliefs. This stems in part from the wide geographical separation of many African peoples, each of whom naturally developed their own local mythology. The other important factor is that African myths were not written down until the nineteenth and twentieth centuries. Before this, for many millennia, myths passed from one generation to another orally. Each new telling tended to be a tiny bit different than the one before, and over the course of the centuries this led to significant alteration and colorful diversity. And part of this diver-

sity was that the monsters of African mythology took many and varied forms.

Yet at least some common mythological themes, including the kinds of monsters inhabiting the myths, occur across most of black Africa. A majority of African peoples, for instance, have creation myths that involve a creator god who shapes the world and then fades from view. Most also feature tricksters—usually animals such as spiders and rabbits, which have little physical strength and prowess and use their wits to survive. The more common forms taken by monsters in these myths are witches, who are usually pictured as evil; evil spirits, who are often the ghosts of dead people; imps (evil fairies) and evil dwarves and trolls; and serpents or other monsters that lived in the forest or in streams or lakes.

The Stubborn Young Girl

Another kind of monster inhabiting the myths of most black African cultures is the human who can transform him- or herself into an animal. The beast-man is usually a devious sort who preys on humans by

This giant bird, known as Nunda, is one of the monsters of Swahili mythology, popular in eastern Africa.

tricking them in some way and then devouring them. A clear example is the shape-shifter that appears in male form in the following myth from Kenya (in east-central Africa, south of Ethiopia), variants of which were told in Zambia and Malawi (both situated south of Kenya).

There was once a young girl of marriageable age whose parents were eager to see her wed and give them grandchildren. However, she was strong-willed, stubborn, and very picky; she steadfastly refused to accept any of the many young men her parents arranged to call on her. Why would she not graciously accept the offer of one of the fine suitors they had brought to see her? the girl's father asked. Other young girls were quick to follow age-old custom and did not give their parents such grief, he said. In fact, he told her, he and her mother had become the laughingstock of the village. The daughter responded by saying that she was sorry. She did not mean to be obstinate, but she just wanted to be happy, and there was no doubt in her mind that none of the suitors she had met so far would have made her so. She went on to promise that she would accept and marry the right man if and when he appeared.

This was not good enough for the parents. They decided

that their daughter would marry the next eligible suitor that came along, regardless of her feelings. It so happened that the village was preparing to hold a festive dance, which was to be attended by young men from neighboring villages. The parents felt that this would be the perfect opportunity to find a suitable young man for their daughter. So they forced her to attend the affair, even though she insisted that she wanted to stay home.

As it turned out, the girl was happy that she did go to the dance. There, she met a young man who was so handsome that most people could not keep themselves from staring at him. He was tall, upright, muscular, and had an irresistible smile and magnetic personality. The girl longed to get to know this striking young man and was delighted when he invited her to dance with him. By the end of the evening she had fallen in love with him.

Shape-shifters and beast-people are popular in African myths. This drawing from the eighteenth century shows a "mere-maid," half-woman and half ape.

And when she, her parents, and her brother returned home, she joyfully told them that the young man had asked her to marry him.

The parents, who were naturally overjoyed at this news, embraced their daughter. But then her brother, who had been unusually quiet all evening, stepped forward and urged them to be cautious. He explained that earlier in the evening he had had occasion to get very close to this fellow during the dancing, and that he had seen something that had made his stomach turn. When the girl and her parents asked what it was that had upset him, he answered that he had seen what appeared to be a second mouth hidden under the hair on the back of the young man's head.

In the Monster's Grasp

Hearing about this so-called second mouth, the father exclaimed that it was the silliest thing he had heard in a very long time; the mother agreed. Everyone grew up learning to beware of the beast-man, the evil shape-shifter, the mother admitted, but surely no one as obviously handsome and charming as this young man could be evil. Everyone in the family, including grandparents, nephews, nieces, and cousins, echoed the mother's opinion and flatly dismissed the brother's story. The young girl and her new suitor wed a week later in front of everyone in the village and then departed to the north, the direction of the young man's village, where they planned to live.

The girl's brother was still suspicious of the young man, though, and he followed the couple at a distance, making sure they did not see him. After about an hour, the young man asked his new bride if she could still see the smoke rising from her father's house. She looked back and replied matter-of-factly that she could, although just barely. After another hour had passed, the husband inquired if she could still see the tops of the hills that lay near her village. Again, she answered affirmatively.

Finally, after almost three hours had elapsed, the couple stopped and looked back again; meanwhile, the brother watched and listened from a nearby hiding place. This time the husband asked if his wife could make out any landmark or vestige of her former home. No, she answered, she could see nothing of her village or the hills near it. But why, she demanded to know, did he keep asking her such strange questions? The young man suddenly hunched over, as if something was forcing his back to bend, and he bared his teeth and began to drool. In a voice that was becoming increasingly husky and menacing, he told her that he wanted to make sure that she would have no chance of running home before he killed and ate her. Before the girl's astonished eyes (and also those of her brother), the husband underwent a frightening transformation. His hands turned into paws, a thick coat of coarse hair grew all over his body, and his once handsome face elongated into the muzzle of a grotesque hyenalike creature.

The girl turned to run, but the monster leapt forward and easily caught up to her. It held her down and howled loudly as spittle dripped in a disgusting stream from his open jaws and slithering tongue. Now the woman would die, the creature exclaimed, and it placed its huge mouth around her delicate neck, preparing to snap it. At that moment, however, the girl was surprised to feel the monster's grip loosen and hear it suck in its breath in a sudden whoosh. Staggering backward, the beast-man clawed at its back, trying to get at an arrow that protruded from a deep wound near its spine. In vain it struggled to dislodge the lethal missile. It finally rolled to the ground, endured a gruesome death spasm, and perished.

Pulling herself to her feet, the girl turned to see her brother approaching, holding his trusty bow. As she embraced him, she admitted that she should have listened to him in the first place. It was a good thing, she added, that he had turned out to be even more stubborn than she. They laughed as he prepared to drag the creature's carcass as a trophy back to the village. In the years that followed, the brother was seen as a hero and a wise

man. And his sister was more careful than ever about choosing just the right young man to marry.

The Cruel Imp

Another tale about a devious creature tricking an innocent young girl was told by a number of peoples who inhabited several coastal regions of eastern Africa, but who spoke a common language, Swahili. The brief story is told here by University of London scholar Geoffrey Parrinder:

This illustration depicts an episode from a Swahili myth in which a gazelle vanquishes several serpents.

The Gazelle cuts off the Serpent's Heads

A girl found a beautiful shell on the seashore, and put it on a rock while she went on with her companions to look for more. Then she forgot it till they were nearly home, and asked her friends to go back with her. They refused and she had to go on alone, in the dangerous dusk, so she sang to keep her courage up. On the rock she found a fairy, and when he heard her he asked her to come closer and sing the song again. Then he seized the girl and stuffed her into a barrel. He went along from village to village, offering to play wonderful music in exchange for a good meal. When the fairy beat the barrel like a drum, the girl sang inside and people gave him plenty of food, but he gave none to the girl.

In time he reached the girl's own village. They had already heard of his fame and begged him to give them an entertainment. When the girl sang, her parents recognized her voice, so they gave the fairy a great deal of wine afterwards to make him fall asleep. They rescued the girl, and put bees and soldier ants into the barrel, so that when the fairy next beat it he would be severely stung.[23]

Similar versions of this story of a cruel imp imprisoning and exploiting a young girl come from the Xosa and Lesotho peoples of southern Africa. In one of these alternate versions, the parents put poisonous snakes into the barrel instead of bees and ants; the snakes bite the imp and he dies.

Another version adds a sort of shape-shifter to the story. This telling has the imp jump into a deep pool of water in an effort to escape the snakes. The imp drowns, and over time a strange pumpkin tree sprouts and grows from the bottom of the pool. Years later some boys who are playing in the area see that the tree has produced some large but misshapen pumpkins, and they take the biggest of the lot home. Their parents, however, having heard the legend of the evil imp who spawned the tree, get an ax and chop the pumpkin into hundreds of pieces.

The Witch and the Crocodile

The peoples of the Ivory Coast, in western Africa, have their own tales of young girls who are menaced by shape-shifting monsters. One of these involves an evil witch who can be described as a beast-woman because she could change herself into an animal. To be more precise, the witch was able, while she was sleeping, to transfer her soul into an animal's body. Having taken possession of the beast, the witch would direct it to go out and commit mischief, mayhem, and murder. No one knew that the animals that caused these troubles were controlled by the witch. In fact, no one in the witch's village even knew

The story of the witch who turned herself into a crocodile drew on the fact that crocodiles, like the one seen here, are among the most feared animals in Africa.

that she was a witch; in the daytime she pretended to be a normal woman, and she had a hard-working husband, who, of course, had no idea of her real identity. She had changed herself into animals on many occasions, mainly because she enjoyed doing evil things, and it was easier to get away with them when in the form of a beast.

One night the witch waited until her husband had gone to sleep and then sneaked out of their hut and made her way to a cave in the forest. There, she went to sleep. Soon, her evil soul rose from her body and drifted out of the cave. The witch's soul traveled through the treetops searching for an animal to inhabit, preferably one that was large and capable of

doing considerable damage to both humans and other animals. Eventually the witch spied a crocodile lumbering through the underbrush on its way to the river. This would be a perfect vehicle for her, she thought. A crocodile has huge jaws, many sharp teeth, a great appetite, and a big belly, which would make her a monster to be reckoned with!

The witch's soul entered the crocodile, which immediately went on a killing spree. At first it devoured only animals, including some tasty lizards and rabbits. But these only whet its appetite and soon the creature began searching for human victims, believing that human flesh would be even more tasty. It found a hut on the outskirts of a nearby village, crawled inside, and ate an entire family, consisting of two parents, a grandmother, and four children.

The witch, in her reptilian form, enjoyed her grisly feast so much that she desired even more human flesh. Her appetite became so great, in fact, that she allowed it to cloud her judgment, a mistake that eventually led to her ruin. Instead of returning to her body in the cave when the sun began to rise, which was her usual practice, she decided to remain in the crocodile's body a while longer so that she could find a few more humans to devour. As the morning progressed, the witch saw a young girl wading into the river to bathe. Slithering silently into the water, the crocodile slowly and carefully approached the unsuspecting girl until it was only a few feet away; then it lunged forward and snatched her in its jaws, intending to drag her away to a secluded grove of trees and eat her.

The Good Counterbalances the Evil

Although African religion and myths contain many witches and other evil beings and monsters, they also feature benevolent gods and forces of good to counterbalance and punish their wickedness. This is anthropologist James W. Telch's description (quoted in editor Mircea Eliade's *Essential Sacred Writings from Around the World*) of the supreme being of the Isoko, a people of southern Nigeria.

Isoko religion begins with Cghene, the Supreme Being, who is believed to have created the world and all peoples, including the Isoko. He lives in the sky, which is part of him, sends rain and sunshine, and shows his anger through thunder. Cghene is entirely beyond human comprehension, has never been seen, is sexless, and is only known by his actions, which have led men to speak of Cghene as "him," because he is thought of as the creator and therefore father of all the Isokos. He is spoken of as Our Father, never as My Father. Cghene always punishes evil and rewards good, a belief that leads the Isokos to blame witchcraft for any evil which may happen to a good man. As, however, Cghene is so distant and unknowable, he has no temples or priests, and no prayers or sacrifices are offered to him directly. To bridge the gulf between himself and man, Cghene appointed an intermediary, called oyise, which is referred to as uko Cghene, or "messenger of Cghene." This oyise is a pole about eight feet long made from the oyise tree, erected after a seven-fold offering [sacrifice] to Cghene, in the compound of the oldest member of the family, and only in his. Before this pole, the family elder throws his used chewing stick each morning and offers prayer for the family and town. Through oyise, Cghene can be invoked in case of calamity or need.

This photo of three Zulu warriors was taken in British South Africa about the year 1900. At the time, the tale of the river monster was still widely-told in their land.

At that same moment, however, a young man from the girl's village happened by on his way to fell some trees with an ax. Seeing the girl struggling to free herself from the great reptile's grasp, he bounded forward into the water and buried his ax into the creature's head. The crocodile immediately let go of its victim, thrashed about for a few seconds, and then died and sank to the bottom of the river. The relieved young girl and her rescuer had no way of knowing that the creature was inhabited by a witch, nor that the witch's soul did not have time to escape its temporary home before the creature died. Therefore, at the very instant of the croc-

odile's death, the witch's body, which was still lying in the cave, died too. The witch's husband never knew why or how his wife had disappeared, and no one found her remains since they were quickly devoured by rats and other scavenging creatures.

A Monster Gives a Lesson in Courtesy

Other monsters besides killer crocodiles lurked in African rivers. According to a myth of the Zulus, who lived in southern Africa, a local river was once infested with a huge monster that was said to be female (although it had a long beard) and to have a humped back. The elders of the village nearest the river warned people not to go near the riverbank, lest the creature jump out and grab them. In particular, the chief of the village admonished his only daughter to stay away from the river.

But the chief's daughter was strong-willed and rebellious, and she felt that her father was too strict. Telling several of her friends that her father and the elders were greatly exaggerating the danger, she convinced the girls to go swimming with her in the river. One sunny day they went to the riverbank. Removing their clothes, they placed them on a large flat rock and dove into the water. After frolicking about for almost an hour, the girls decided that they had had enough and climbed out onto the riverbank. When they got to the big rock, though, their clothes were gone!

Suddenly, the girls were startled by a strange voice coming from behind a thick grove of marsh grass, a voice that asked them if they were looking for their clothes. As they watched, the river monster emerged from the grove. It was larger than the largest of the huts in the village, had a huge, hideous hump on its back, and walked on four wide, webbed feet that left massive impressions in the soft mud along the bank. The beast was carrying the girls' clothes in its claws. It told them that it would be willing to return their clothes on one condition— namely, that they ask for them in a polite way. After all, they had not asked for permission to swim in the river,

which was the creature's home. The least they could do, it said, was to be courteous now.

One by one, the girls apologized for invading the monster's privacy and politely asked for their clothes. In each case, the creature dutifully returned the garments. The only exception was the chief's daughter, who remained as strong-willed and rebellious as ever. Why should she be polite to an ugly, filthy monster? she asked. It had taken her clothes, she said, and it must now give them back and be quick about it! At this, the creature suddenly became angry. It lunged forward, grabbed the impertinent girl, who was now sorry for her discourtesy, and dragged her away into the river.

Running as fast as they could, the other girls returned to the village and told the chief what had happened. He ordered ten of his best warriors to hurry to the river, kill the monster, and rescue his daughter. But when they attacked the beast, it grabbed them and swallowed them whole. Now angrier than ever, the monster climbed out of the water and strode to the village, where it swallowed every living thing in sight, even the cows, chickens, and dogs.

One man managed to escape, however. He had seen his entire family swallowed by the monster, and he was not about to allow the creature to escape back to the river without a fight. Arming himself with a spear and a large club, the man chased the monster, which tried to hide behind trees and rocks along the way. But each time the beast dropped out of sight, the man asked an animal (a buffalo, a leopard,

The Wisdom of the Zulus

Many myths about monsters feature a moral lesson or a kernel of wisdom that will hopefully influence people to be wise, constructive, and/or adhere to socially acceptable behavior. The Zulu tale of the river monster, for example, contains a lesson about the importance of courtesy. Among other things (including the skill and valor of their warriors), the Zulus were known for their social wisdom, as evidenced by some of their wise sayings (quoted here from editor Alvin M. Josephy Jr.'s *The Horizon History of Africa*).

1. *A man is not stabbed with one spear. [A man worthy of the name should not fall down with the first thrust of the spear.]*

2. *He who installs a king never rules with him. [Kings have short memories and tend to forget the people who helped them in the days when they were not kings.]*

3. *He cries with one eye. [He pretends to be sorry when he is not.]*

4. *The sheep has killed an elephant. [The impossible has happened.]*

5. *There is no frog that does not peep out of its pool. [Everyone will take a chance in the hope that he will succeed.]*

The Zulus were known for their skill and ferocity in battle. This nineteenth-century drawing shows a Zulu war dance.

6. *No buffalo was ever beaten by its calf. [Old people are usually far more experienced than the young.]*

7. *Days are things that want to be provided for. [One has to make proper provision for the bad days.]*

8. *One does not follow a snake into its hole. [It is not wise to take unnecessary risks.]*

9. *He holds the spear by the blade. [A person who has been bragging gives himself away by doing a foolish thing.]*

10. *A king is a king because of the people. [A king is no king if he has no followers.]*

and an elephant in succession) to point out where it was hiding. Finally, the man caught up with the monster in a field. Taking careful aim, he threw his spear into the creature's hump, which was apparently a vital spot, for it fell on the ground gravely wounded. The man finished the monster off by using the club to crush its skull.

Seconds later, all of the people and animals the beast had devoured that day crawled out of its mouth. Each thanked the man who had slain the monster. The last one out was the chief's stubborn daughter, who wasted no time in apologizing profusely to everyone. Thereafter, she was the most obedient and polite young woman in all of Zululand.

That this story had a strong moral—about the importance of children being obedient and polite—is surely no accident. The tale of the beast-man marrying the stubborn girl also had a moral: that a young girl should listen to the advice of her parents or else face dire consequences. The African myths were passed along orally from village to village and from generation to generation, repeatedly changing to fit the needs of local villages and regions. In this way, myths and folktales acquired new meanings over time.

Ancient Scandinavia: Dragons and Giants in a Bleak World

According to the myths of the Norse (or Northmen, some of whom are known today as the Vikings), fearsome monsters lurked beneath the earth. As was the case with monsters in India's myths, the monsters frequently opposed and battled the gods. A major difference, however, is the ultimate outcome of such ongoing conflicts. In Indian mythology, as in the myths of the Greeks and many other peoples, good is usually expected to triumph over evil ultimately, whether it be in the near future or perhaps at the end of time. So there is, more often than not, a somewhat hopeful, optimistic tone running through most world mythologies.

By contrast, Norse mythology is pervaded by a decidedly bleak and pessimistic outlook. In most of the myths told by the Norse, the gods do manage to win over their opponents. But these victories are in a sense rendered meaningless, for in looking at the stories in the collective sense, it is clear that the gods have no chance in the long run of defeating all of the monsters or of overcoming the forces of evil and chaos. According to Norse belief, in the far future there will come Ragnarok, "the Twilight of the Gods." This event was seen as the final conflict between the gods and their gruesome enemies, and this battle the gods would lose. About this seemingly hopeless view of the future, Edith Hamilton writes,

> The world of Norse mythology is a strange world. Asgard, the home of the gods, is unlike any other heaven men have dreamed of. No radiancy of joy is in it, no assurance of bliss. It is a grave and solemn place, over which hangs the threat of an inevitable doom. The gods know that a day will come when they will be destroyed. . . . Asgard will fall in ruins. The cause the forces of good are fighting to defend against the forces of evil is hopeless. Nevertheless, the gods will fight for it to the end. Necessarily, the same is true of humanity. If the gods are finally helpless before evil, men and women must be more so. . . . In the last battle between good and evil, they will fight on the side of the gods and die with them.[24]

This desolate, discouraging outlook pervading Norse religion and its attendant myths may have derived at least in part from the fact that the Norse themselves often faced unusually bleak lives. As the name *Northmen* suggests, they

This imaginative drawing by Johannes Gehrts depicts Ragnarok, the ultimate battle at the end of time when the forces of evil will destroy the Norse gods.

lived in Europe's far northern reaches, inhabiting Scandinavia and later Iceland and other islands of the cold northern seas. In these places they endured long, cruel winters; the growing seasons of their crops were short, so food was often scarce; and farmsteads and villages were commonly separated by a dozen or more miles, so many people had to learn to deal with isolation and loneliness. In short, life was a constant struggle for existence.

The uncertainty of Norse life was bound to stimulate the development of superstition and a belief in monsters and evil forces. At the same time, it forced people and the heroes they envisioned to be tough and capable of enduring hardship. As the noted scholar of the Norse H. R. Ellis Davidson phrases it,

> They were very conscious of the grim underworld where giants and monsters dwelt, and of the constant threat to their precarious little world once the forces of chaos were unleashed. Their experience of a savage world in which kingdoms were constantly set up and destroyed, with a background of stormy seas and long cold winter nights, gave a somber tinge to their picture of the realm of the gods, but also imparted a sturdy vigor to the figures who people their myths.[25]

In the Norse worldview, monsters most often took the form of giants, serpents, and dragons. (The huge wolf called Fenrir was a notable exception.) All manner of giants were thought to populate nature, some living underground, others inside mountains, under the sea, or even within clouds. Sometimes giants could be friendly; more often they were a menace or a threat to people and the gods. The Norse fascination with serpents and dragons can be seen in their art and in the design of their ships, both of which often featured carved wooden dragon heads. Serpents and dragons had powerful religious significance, too. In Scandinavia, says Davidson,

> the dragon came to be regarded as the guardian of the grave mound, watching over its treasures. Sometimes it is implied that he [the

A carved dragon head that once decorated the prow of a Viking ship. The dragon was an ever-present motif in Norse life and lore.

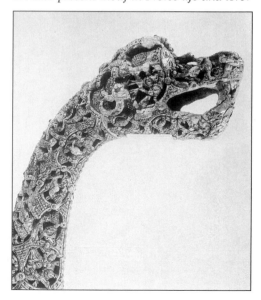

Odin: A Strange and Solemn Figure

The chief god of the Norse, Odin, plays a prominent role in many of the Scandinavian myths. From her classic book about mythology, noted scholar Edith Hamilton describes him.

He is a strange and solemn figure, always aloof. Even when he sits at the feasts of the gods in his golden palace, Gladsheim, or with the heroes in Valhalla [a hall in Asgard where the souls of dead heroes reside], he eats nothing. The food set before him he gives to the two wolves who crouch at his feet. On his shoulders perch two ravens, who fly each day through the world and bring him back news of all that men do. The name of the one is Thought (Hugin) and of the other Memory (Munin). While the other gods feasted, Odin pondered on what Thought and Memory taught him. He had the responsibility more than all the other gods together of postponing as long as possible the day of doom, Ragnarok, when heaven and earth would be destroyed. He was the All-father, supreme among gods and men, yet even so he constantly sought for more wisdom.

He went down to the Well of Wisdom [lying beneath one of the roots of the great tree that supposedly supported the world], guarded by [a wise being named] Mimir . . . to beg for a drink from it, and when Mimir answered that he must pay for it with one of his eyes, Odin consented to lose the eye. . . . He imperiled his life again to take away from the giants the skaldic mead ["beer of poets"], which made anyone who tasted it a poet. This good gift he bestowed upon men as well as upon the gods. In all ways he was mankind's benefactor.

A nineteenth-century engraving shows the great Norse god Odin sitting on his thrown and attended by his trusty wolves.

dragon] is to be identified with the dead man buried in the mound, and in some of the late legendary sagas it is said that after death a man became a dragon and guarded the treasure which he had taken into the grave with him. . . . The serpent-dragon . . . has left its mark in the serpentine ornament and the constantly reiterated [repeated] snake-motif upon memorial stones raised over the dead. The snake as a symbol of the world of the dead is as recurrent in the art of the north as in its literature.[26]

The sagas and literature to which Davidson refers are the original sources of the Norse myths. Of the three main surviving sources, the first is the *Poetic Edda* (or *Elder Edda*), an anonymous compilation of myths dating from about A.D. 1300. A copy of it was discovered in an Icelandic farmhouse in the seventeenth century. There are also the *Prose Edda* (or *Younger Edda*), a work by a thirteenth-century Icelandic chieftain, Snorri Sturlson; and a history of Denmark written in the twelfth century by a Dane named Saxo Grammaticus.[27]

The Death of Otter

Snorri's *Prose Edda* is the source of the story of Fafnir, a man who was transformed into a monstrous dragon. Fafnir was one of the three sons of a well-to-do man named Hreidmar. One day Hreidmar heard some-

one knocking at the front door of his large house, and when he answered it he saw three very tall, muscular, bearded men standing on his doorstep— or at least they appeared to be men. In reality, the three were gods—Odin, god of war and ruler of Asgard; Hoenir, Odin's silent but loyal and athletic companion; and Loki, the trickster, who often changed himself into various animals and caused mischief. The visitors told Hreidmar that they had been out for a walk in the woods and needed a place to rest for the night; being a hospitable man, Hreidmar invited them in.

Soon it was suppertime and Fafnir and his brother Regin joined their father and the three strangers at the long table in Hreidmar's dining hall. As the men ate, they conversed, and at some point Loki bragged about a deed he had performed earlier that day. When they had paused by a nearby waterfall, Loki began, they had seen an otter eating a salmon on the edge of the stream. Loki had flung a rock at the otter and killed it, so he had managed to catch both a salmon and an otter with a single rock!

On hearing this story, Hreidmar and his sons leapt to their feet. Hreidmar called Loki an ignorant fool, not realizing of course that he was addressing a god. The otter he had slain was the old man's third son, who possessed the ability to take the form of an animal when it suited him. Loki looked at Odin, who was as surprised as he was. How could they have known the otter was actually human? Loki asked. Hreidmar answered that this was of no consequence now, that what mattered was that the strangers must make amends for killing his son.

Speaking for his companions as well as for himself, Odin agreed to compensate the man and his surviving sons for their loss. Hreidmar demanded that the visitors pay him as much gold as it would take to fill the dead otter's skin and enough additional gold to bury the stuffed skin so thoroughly that not even a single whisker would be visible. This was a tall order. But not long after he had begun searching for gold, Loki chanced on a dwarf named Andvari, who lived deep in the forest.

The Norse god Odin travels through Midgard, the land of humans.

Andvari was a greedy character who had managed, through both legal and illegal means, to accumulate a large cache of treasure, including a great deal of gold. Being a god, Loki had little trouble overpowering Andvari and confiscating his treasure.

Loki was just about to leave the dwarf's lair when he noticed a beautiful gold ring on Andvari's finger. The god demanded that the dwarf hand over the ring, but Andvari frowned, took a step backward, and refused. Loki must not take the ring, the dwarf said, because it bore a curse that would bring bad luck and destruction on anyone who owned it. Andvari explained that he himself had not believed in the curse at first, but that now he did since it had caused him to lose everything of value that he owned. Loki merely laughed. The dwarf was being ridiculous, he said, for the real reason he was losing his treasure was because Loki was strong enough to take it from him. And anyway, Loki pointed out, even if there was a curse, Loki would surely be immune since he was a god.

The Sword and the Dragon

Loki was wrong on both points: The ring was indeed cursed, and his divine powers did not make him immune. Luckily for him, he escaped the curse because he did not take permanent possession of the ring but instead used it to cover the last of the otter's whiskers still showing when he and Odin buried the corpse in gold. Odin told Hreidmar that the old man had now been

This Norse forge stone, found in Denmark, is incised with the face of the god Loki, one of the most influential and unpredictable of the gods.

fairly compensated for the loss of his son and said his good-byes. Hreidmar nodded, seemingly satisfied, and saw the three visitors to the door. He said that if the strangers happened to come by next year they would hardly recognize the place, for he planned to use his newfound fortune to enlarge his home and to build a new barn.

But Hreidmar never ended up enjoying the treasure, for the curse of the gold ring began to manifest itself almost immediately. First, his sons Fafnir and Regin were overcome with the desire to possess the gold, and after planning to divide the

spoils evenly between them, they killed their father. Once Hreidmar was out of the way, Fafnir turned on his brother and refused to honor their bargain. Regin objected that Fafnir had broken his word. And even though they were brothers, Regin warned, he would fight to gain his fair share of the riches.

At that moment, Fafnir grinned and informed Regin that he would have no chance of defeating him in a fight. This was because there was something that neither Regin nor their father had known: Fafnir, like their dead brother, had the ability to change himself into a beast. Indeed, before Regin's astonished gaze, Fafnir transformed himself into a monstrous dragon with a thick hide covered by glistening scales, a long powerful tail, and a mouthful of huge, pointed teeth. The dragon lumbered over to the treasure, sat on it, and leered at Regin, as if challenging him to try and take some.

Realizing that he was no match for a dragon, Regin left his home and journeyed beyond the mountains that enclosed his valley. His goal was to find the famous young hero Sigurd the Volsung to deal with Fafnir. As it happened, Sigurd was uniquely qualified to dispatch a beast like Fafnir. Sigurd's father, Sigmund, had been given a splendid and powerful sword by Odin. In his time Sigmund had been a hero and had used the sword to fight Odin's enemies; however, the weapon had been broken in two shortly before Sigmund's death in battle. Sigurd had kept the pieces of the sword, planning to rejoin them when a need for the fabulous weapon arose. Once Regin found him and told him about the dragon, such a need seemed at hand. Sigurd and Regin reforged the mighty sword, making it whole once more, and rode off toward Regin's home.

When they reached their destination, Sigurd and Regin carefully observed the dragon, Fafnir, from a safe distance. Most of the time, it sat on the treasure, keeping a watchful eye out for anyone who might come too near. Once each day, however, the huge creature left its vigil and crawled down to a nearby stream to drink. This proved its undoing. Sigurd waited till the beast was back on top of the treasure, dug a deep pit beside the stream, covered the top of the pit with branches, and waited inside. The next time the dragon approached the stream for its daily drink, it stood over the pit, and Sigurd stabbed it from below, killing it.

Then, fortunately for Sigurd, a strange and marvelous thing happened. When he

A 1909 painting from a book about Norse myths shows the hero Sigurd slaying Fafnir, a man who turned himself into a fearsome dragon.

was roasting the dragon's heart in preparation for eating it, he burned his finger on the organ. As he put the finger into his mouth to soothe it, a drop of the dragon's blood touched his tongue, and suddenly he found that he had the ability to understand the speech of animals. Two birds that were sitting on a tree branch above him warned him that Regin was worried that he might take some of the treasure and was planning to kill him. Sure enough, when Sigurd turned around, he saw the other man with a long dagger raised to strike. In one swift and masterful move, Sigurd swung his father's wondrous sword, parting Regin's head from his body, which collapsed into the dirt. The hero then proceeded to load the treasure—including the ring and its attendant curse—onto his horse and depart.

The Unpredictable and Changeable Loki

In this excerpt from his popular mythological dictionary, noted art historian Philip Wilkinson tells about the enigmatic Loki, who killed the otter who turned out to be Fafnir's brother and who also fathered three of the most terrible monsters known to the Norse.

The god Loki, a shape-changer, is shown here, as a horse.

Part god and part giant, Loki was a mixture of trickster and creator. He could be a friend of the gods, but Loki also caused the death of Balder [Odin's son and the most handsome of all of the gods]. He led his monstrous children and the souls of the dead against the gods in Ragnarok [the final battle between the gods and their enemies], and therefore they were wary of him. His other names included the Sly God and the Father of Lies. The name Loki means "fire." According to one myth, Loki was created when his father Farbauti struck a flint and made a spark, which flew into the undergrowth of the island of Laufey, and fire—Loki—was born. Like fire, Loki was unpredictable and changeable. A miraculous shape-changer, he could appear as a bird, a fish, a fly, a giant, even as a puff of smoke.

The mighty Norse god Thor is pictured with his famous hammer in this nineteenth-century engraving.

The Largest Giant Threatens Asgard

Heroes like Sigmund and Sigurd could be counted on to defeat dragons and other threatening creatures in the short run. The problem, of course, was that in the long run all of the heroes would die and their opponents would inherit the earth. This was even true of one of the greatest of the gods, who, like Sigurd, used a fabulous weapon to dispatch a monster. In this case, it was not a sword but rather the mighty hammer belonging to Thor, the deity of thunder. He was one of the largest

and most powerful Norse gods, and his hammer, which had been forged by dwarves, had crushed many an enemy of the gods and humans.

The story begins when Thor was away from Asgard on a mission to rid the world of some pesky trolls. Thor's colleague, Odin, leader of the gods, was out one day riding his magical horse, Sleipnir. A gift from Loki, the trickster, Sleipnir had eight legs and could gallop almost as fast as the wind, which gave Odin a tremendous advantage in battling his enemies.

Suddenly Odin encountered Hrungnir, who was monstrous even as giants go. Hrungnir was not only the largest giant (towering six or seven times Odin's height), but he also had a head and heart made of stone, which made him very formidable in a fight. Hrungnir told Odin that the steed he was riding was the weirdest-looking horse he had ever seen. In a mean, sarcastic tone of voice, the giant asked if the horse had trouble walking with all of those extra legs. Odin answered that this was Sleipnir, who had no trouble walking. In fact, the god bragged, there was not a faster horse in all of the universe.

Hrungnir took exception to Odin's claim. The giant pointed at his own steed,

Odin rides his loyal and magical horse Sleipnir in this scene carved on an eighth-century Viking stele (marker or ceremonial stone).

which was, like himself, huge in size, and he claimed that it could easily outrun Odin's steed. Hrungnir challenged Odin to a race, saying that the first to reach the borders of Asgard would win; Odin accepted this challenge. The two readied themselves, then sped away over the mountaintops. At first Odin and Sleipnir outdistanced their opponents, but after a while Hrungnir and his gigantic horse pulled ahead.

Reaching Asgard first, Hrungnir surprised the other gods, who were not used to having giants drop in on them uninvited. Yet with the mighty Thor absent, no god felt up to the task of fighting the monstrous intruder. So no one did any-

thing when Hrungnir got drunk and began swaggering around and insulting and threatening the deities. The gods were not nearly as tough as their reputation, he said, and he proceeded to brag about how he could easily wreck the place. In fact, he said, he was thinking seriously about sinking Asgard beneath the sea, carrying off Thor's wife, Sif, and forcing her to serve him. In the face of this threat, the gods, including Odin, who had just arrived on Sleipnir, surrounded Sif to protect her and prepared to fight.

This became unnecessary, however, for at that moment the great Thor came bounding into Asgard, furious that a giant had entered and threatened the abode of the gods. While standing on a large rock to make up for the difference in height between himself and Hrungnir, Thor demanded that the giant leave at once. But Hrungnir retorted that Thor was a puny fellow who did not frighten him in the least. If the gods wanted to get rid of him, he said, they would have to fight him; Hrungnir made it clear, though, that he doubted they had the courage to do so. Incensed by this insult, Thor stepped forward so that he and the giant were almost nose to nose. In a loud voice, the thunder god accepted the challenge and warned that the giant would soon feel his wrath. Hrungnir laughed and said that he would grind Thor's wrath in the dirt, then destroy Asgard and make off with Sif.

The fight that ensued was one of the most memorable in the annals of Asgard. All of the gods gathered around to give Thor moral support; likewise, a large number of giants arrived to cheer on Hrungnir. Based on her reading of Snorri Sturlson's *Prose Edda,* Davidson describes the battle this way:

> For this duel the giants made a clay man, called Mist-Calf, to support Hrungnir. Hrungnir himself . . . was armed with a stone shield and a whetstone [a stone used to sharpen sword blades]. Thor came out with Thialfi [a swift-footed human follower who had been traveling with him] to meet the giant, and Thialfi [who pretended to turn on Thor and

give helpful advice to Hrungnir] told Hrungnir that he had better stand on his shield, in case Thor attacked him from below. Then Thor bore down on Hrungnir with thunder and lightning, and hurled his hammer at him, while the giant threw his whetstone. The weapons met in mid air, and the whetstone was shattered, but one piece lodged in Thor's forehead. The hammer went on to strike Hrungnir's skull and break it in pieces.[28]

Seeing the biggest and meanest of their number fall dead before the victorious Thor, the other giants ran for their lives. As for Thor, he recovered fully from the wound made by the whetstone fragment entering his head. However, that fragment would remain lodged inside his skull, a reminder of his triumph over a monster that might have destroyed Asgard.

Loki's Monstrous Children

There were other monsters in the world in those days besides dragons and giants. Perhaps the most famous and feared of these were Loki's monstrous children— the World Serpent (also called the Midgard Serpent), Hel, and Fenrir. He sired these creatures when he was passing through the land of the frost giants, which lay far to the north of Asgard. In that faraway region, Loki met and coupled with a giantess named Angrboda,

The Twilight of the Gods

This portion of the Norse *Poetic Edda* (translated by Henry A. Bellows) describes Ragnarok, "the Twilight of the Gods."

Over the sea from the north there sails a ship
With the people of Hel [the dead], at the helm stands Loki;
After the wolf [Loki's monstrous wolf-son, Fenrir] do wild men follow,
And with them the brother of Byleist [Loki] goes.
Surt [a fire giant] fares from the south with the scourge of branches,
The sun of the battle-gods shone from his sword;
The crags [mountains] are sundered [broken], the giant-women sink,
The dead throng the way to the underworld, and heaven is cloven [cut in two]. . . .
In anger smites [strikes] the warder of the earth—
Forth from their homes must all men flee—
Nine paces fares the son of Fjorgyn [the god Thor],
And, slain by the [World] Serpent, fearless he sinks.
The sun turns black, earth sinks in the sea,
The hot stars down from heaven are whirled;
Fierce grows the steam and the life-feeding flame,
Till fire leaps high about heaven itself.
Now Fenrir howls loud . . . the fetters will burst, and the wolf run free;
Much do I know, and more can see
Of the fate of the gods, the mighty in [the] fight [to end all fights].

whose name means "Foreteller of Grief." This name was well earned, for soon after the gods learned of the birth of Loki's offspring, they also discovered that these monsters would one day cause both the gods and the world of humans a great deal of grief. This prediction came from three maidens called the Norns, who possessed the miraculous ability to see into the future. When Ragnarok came in the far future, the Norns told the gods, these monsters would be unleashed on Asgard and the world. One of them would slay the mighty Odin. Another of them would kill the great Thor. Furthermore, the Norns said, there was nothing any of the gods could do to stop these things from happening because what was written by fate could not be unwritten.

Odin, Thor, and the others carefully considered what the Norns had revealed. They knew that these maidens never lied, so the future of the gods did indeed appear bleak. Yet as they always did, the gods refused to give in, even to the inevitable, and they resolved to use both brains and brawn to resist fate and try to create a different, more positive future. Odin ordered his strongest warriors to journey to the land of the frost giants and bring back the monsters Loki had fathered. This they did.

The gods were both disgusted and alarmed when they gazed at these creatures. The first, the serpent, was miles long and had a hideous forked tongue that flittered obscenely when it opened its enormous mouth. Odin wasted no time in grabbing the monster and throwing it into the vast sea that encircled Midgard (the Norse name for the world of the humans). He hoped that the serpent would drown;

This old Norse brooch takes the form of the World Serpent.

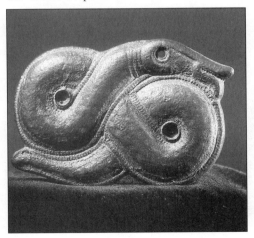

instead, it sank to the bottom and, remaining very much alive, grew even longer, until its body encircled the whole world (hence its name—the World Serpent). According to the prophecy of the Norns, the gigantic creature would remain there, on the world's outer edge, until the advent of Ragnarok, when it would rise to threaten the gods and humans.

After tossing the serpent into the sea, Odin switched his attention to Hel. This female monster was bizarre and repulsive to say the least. The popular modern myth teller Philip Wilkinson describes her as "the queen of the dead. . . . The upper half of her body was alive and flesh-colored, the lower half was dead and black . . . and giving off the smell of rotting flesh."[29] Odin turned to his fellow gods and asked what should be done with this hideous creature. All agreed that Odin should throw Hel down into the depths of Niflheim, the frozen land of the dead, and he immediately did so. The gods were hoping that Hel would be powerless and soon would be forgotten in the distant and somber realm of death. They were wrong; Hel, who was as resilient as the World Serpent, took charge of Niflheim, reorganized it to her liking, and settled down to bide her time and wait patiently for the coming of Ragnarok.

The Chaining of Fenrir

Finally, Odin and his divine companions turned their attention to Loki's third monstrous offspring—Fenrir, an enormous and vicious wolf. Odin explained that he sensed that of the three monsters this one was potentially the most dangerous. And sure enough, one of the Norns confirmed his insight. Fenrir was destined to do both Odin and humanity untold damage, she said. Therefore, he must not simply throw the creature into some faraway place, lulling himself into the false hope that he would thereby be rid of it. Instead, his best course was to keep the great wolf at Asgard, where he could monitor its behavior closely. Moreover, the Norn explained, Fenrir was wild and would not stay confined in Asgard unless Odin bound it securely.

Odin considered the Norn's advice logical and sound. So he ordered his blacksmiths to forge a mighty iron chain and collar and to use these to bind the huge wolf. But as soon as the chain and collar were in place, Fenrir let out a loud howl that sounded like a laugh and easily snapped the iron chain. Smiling, Fenrir exclaimed that Odin would have to do much better than that if he wanted to fetter him. Undaunted, the chief god ordered that a new chain be forged, this one twice as thick and twice as long as the first; the monster, however, which was growing in size and strength by the hour, broke the second one as quickly as the first. A third and even larger

chain suffered the same fate as the first two.

For a while, the gods seemed stumped as to how the monster could be bound securely. Then Odin had an idea. He called forth one of the gods' servants, Skirnir, and ordered him to ride as fast as he could to the land of the dark elves, who possessed special powers of black magic. Skirnir should tell the elves about the gods' predicament and promise that Odin would give them a huge sack of gold if they found a way to bind the wolf.

A few days later Skirnir returned with a magic chain created by the elves. It was

A painting by artist Dorothy Hartley shows the gods attempting to bind the mighty wolf Fenrir.

The god Tyr prepares to put his hand in Fenrir's mouth in a bronze plaque originally mounted on a battle helmet.

made of six things that seemed to have no measurable substance: the roots of a mountain, the beard of a woman, the noise a cat makes when walking, the breath of a fish, the power of a bear, and the spittle of a bird. When the gods brought the narrow and nearly transparent chain to Fenrir, the wolf stared at it in disbelief. It howled that they had to be joking and insisted that such a flimsy thing would never hold it. Odin grinned. If the wolf was so confident that the chain was useless, then why not let the gods fetter him with it? If the chain was truly as weak as Fenrir suspected, he would easily break it.

Fenrir's glowing red eyes narrowed as he considered Odin's offer, and finally the wolf agreed to allow the chief god to bind him with the new chain. But there was a catch to the deal. To show their good faith, one of the gods must put his hand in the wolf's mouth. At this gruesome suggestion, all of the gods took a step backward; all, that is, except for Tyr, the sky god and Odin's son, who was renowned for his courage. Tyr agreed to put his hand in the wolf's great mouth while the others fettered the creature with the silken chain.

As Odin had hoped, the chain made by the elves worked and the monster, which was both surprised and shocked, found that the more it struggled the tighter the chain became. Fenrir was enraged. While the gods were laughing and congratulating themselves for their victory, the beast bit poor Tyr's hand off. Thereafter, gods and humans alike periodically paid homage to Tyr for his sacrifice, and Tyr himself professed that it was a small price to pay for saving the world from its most threatening monster.

But was this perceived safety a mere illusion? Like its loathsome siblings, Fenrir learned to bide its time and wait. Ragnorak, the day of final reckoning, would eventually come, it knew; though the gods and humans had enjoyed many victories over the forces of evil and darkness, those forces were fated to one day have their revenge. And as the all-seeing Norns had told Odin, no matter what the gods did to try to stop the inevitable from occurring, what was written by fate could not be unwritten.

Ancient North America: In the Belly of the Sea Monster

The monsters of Native American mythology and folklore are numerous and highly diverse. This is not surprising considering that Native Americans belong to many different regional groups and tribes with distinct individual cultures. The highly varied physical settings these peoples originally inhabited ranged from the icy wastelands of northern Canada to the temperate, heavily forested lands of the American eastern seaboard; the rolling plains of the Midwest; and the hot, dry deserts of the Southwest, to name only a few.

The result of this wide variety of settings was that separate tribes or regional groups of tribes developed their own distinctive religious views, gods, and myths; and the nature of the monsters and other elements in these myths was heavily colored by their local settings. The Inuit (or Eskimos), who lived near the Bering Sea (in northern Canada), for instance, believed that one of the major predators of that region, the killer whale, could transform itself into a wolf. In that form it supposedly roamed the icy tundra looking for people to eat. By contrast, the Iroquois, who lived in the heavily forested region that is now the northeastern United States, had a myth in which huge supernatural beings, the Stone Giants, regularly uprooted trees to use as weapons. Former University of Nebraska scholar Hartley B. Alexander, a noted expert on Native American cultures, describes some of the wide variety of monstrous beings populating American Indian mythology:

> There are manlike monsters, including giants, dwarfs, cannibals, and hermaphrodites [beings having both male and female sex organs]; animal monsters, bird monsters, water monsters, etc.; composite and malformed creatures, such as one-eyed giants, headless bodies and bodiless heads, skeletons, persons half stone, one-legged, double-headed, and flint-armored beings, harpies [flying creatures with women's faces], witches, ogres, etc. . . . Legends of serpents and giant birds occur especially in descriptions of atmospheric and meteorological [weather-related] phenomena; the story of the hero swallowed by a monster is usually in connection with the origin of animals.[30]

One popular monster from Native American myths, especially those originating in northern Canada, was the killer whale, depicted in this tomb carving.

However, a few of these monster types were particularly common. A great many Indian peoples had stories about monsters consisting of heads without bodies, for instance. And as Alexander points out,

> There is a striking similarity in the personnel of the mythic sea-powers among the Eskimo and on the northwest coast [of what is now the United States], nearly every type of being in the one group having its equivalent in the other—mermen [male mermaids], phantom boat-men . . . living boats, and, most curious of all, the Fire-People. . . . Everywhere there are well-defined groups of underwater beings, some-times reptilian or piscine [fishlike], sometimes human in form. Among the important myths in which underwater monsters are conspicu-ous are: the common legend of a hero swallowed by a huge fish or other creature . . . from whose body he cuts his way to freedom, or is otherwise released; the flood story, in which the hero's brother, or companion, is dragged down to death by water monsters which cause the deluge [great flood] when the hero takes revenge upon them; and the southwestern myth of the subterranean water monster who threatens to inundate the world in revenge for the theft of his two children and who is appeased only by the sacrifice of . . . a youth and a maid.[31]

A modern painting depicts the "great head" of the Iroquois. Disembodied heads are common in Native American myths.

Swallowed by the Sea Monster

Alexander's reference to heroes is impor-tant. As is true of local mythologies from every corner of the globe, the monsters of Native American myths were invariably challenged and almost always defeated by human heroes. These are usually larger-than-life characters who possess special skills or weapons; higher-than-normal strength, endurance, or intelligence; super-natural powers; semidivine heritage; or some combination of these attributes.

Sea monsters are another common creature inhabiting native American lore. This drawing depicts a warrior-hero defeating such a beast.

One of the most entertaining stories of a monster meeting its end at the hands of such a hero comes from the lore of the tribes of the American Northwest. The villain of the piece is a sea beast, one of the more common monsters listed by Alexander; the hero is a young warrior named Stoneribs. According to legend, Stoneribs showed his special abilities almost from the moment of his birth. He could walk and run before he was two, and soon after that he taught himself to string a bow and shoot arrows. His parents and neighbors were amazed to see this young child dashing through the woods and

felling birds and other game like an adult hunter.

Stoneribs also developed some special abilities that no other human possessed. One day when he was about ten, he was out hunting and noticed an eagle carrying a fish in its beak. The great bird dropped the fish, seemingly on purpose, not far from the boy and then flew away. When Stoneribs examined the fish, he saw that it had a strange copper-colored marking on its side. Suddenly an eerie voice issued from a nearby cedar tree. It told Stoneribs to listen carefully. The boy should skin the fish from the tail upward, it instructed, then stretch the skin and allow it to dry in the noonday sun. From this he could fashion a garment that, when worn, would give him many of the powers and abilities of fish. It was a gift, the voice said, from the goddess named Volcano Woman, who was Stoneribs's true mother. Stoneribs did as the voice instructed, turning the fish skin into an outfit. Sure enough, he found that when wearing it he could breath underwater and swim rapidly through the deep, just like a fish.

It was not long after this incident that Stoneribs had occasion to use his newfound gift to aid people in need—something he had always wanted to do. With his unnaturally keen hearing, the boy detected the sound of people crying for help from someplace far to the south of his village. He hurriedly journeyed through forests and across mountains until he reached a village on the seacoast and saw many of the local women kneeling and wailing on the beach. What was the problem? Stoneribs asked one of the women. Why were they crying so loudly and forlornly? The young woman, who was, like the others, unusually thin, replied that there had been nearly nothing to eat for weeks and that they and their children were starving. Also, some of the women were grieving because they had recently become widows. Each time that the village hunters had ventured out in their canoes to bring back fish, the sea monster Qagwaai had capsized the boats and devoured the men. If this kept up, the woman said, her people would all die

and the village would become an empty shell.

Stoneribs could not bear to see such suffering, and he endeavored to help the villagers. One of the women provided him with a canoe, and he paddled out into the nearby bay while some of the surviving men followed in other boats. Fearlessly, Stoneribs stood up in the canoe and yelled the monster's name twelve times. This had the desired effect, for the creature, Qagwaai, which resembled a killer whale, except that it was many times larger, soon surfaced. Seeing the boy in the boat, it immediately swam toward what it assumed was its next victim. Stoneribs quickly strung an arrow on his mighty bow and let loose the shaft, which penetrated the monster's head, causing it to break off its attack. Diving into the water, Stoneribs, who was wearing his magic garment, chased after the beast. Eventually Qagwaai grew weary of the chase, suddenly turned on the boy, and swallowed him whole. But this turned out to be a fatal mistake for the monster. As it dove deeper into the sea, thinking it had won the fight, Stoneribs shot a barrage of deadly arrows, fatally wounding the creature from the inside.

A while later the dead sea monster washed up on the beach, and the villagers warily approached it. To their surprise and relief, a knife blade appeared from its belly and Stoneribs cut his way out and stood, unhurt, before them. The evil Qagwaai would never bother the villagers again, he told them.

The Undersea Kingdom

Another, even more fantastic tale of sea monsters was told by the peoples living farther north, along the Pacific coasts of Canada and Alaska. According to this myth, whalelike sea monsters ruled an undersea kingdom that was in many ways like the world on land. Somehow the creatures' realm had forests, mountains, villages, and so forth. Over the years, many men and women, both young and old, had been snatched by the monsters and taken to this bizarre undersea world; however, none of the humans who had visited this realm had ever returned to tell about it.

No one ever returned from the monster's realm—that is, until the coming of

A shaman's rattle, used to make noise during religious ceremonies, bears the face of a killer whale.

an extraordinary young hunter named Gunarhnesemgyet. It is said that his love for his wife was so great that it endowed him with the tremendous strength, fortitude, and craftiness needed to face and defeat the monsters. The adventure of this young couple began when Gunarhnesemgyet killed a sea otter, skinned it, and gave it to his wife to clean. She went down to the beach and commenced washing the skin. At one point she accidentally stepped onto the skin with both of her feet and, to her dismay, found herself drifting out to sea on it. It was not long before one of the sea monsters, which was patrolling the shore looking for victims, saw her and swam up from beneath, capturing the woman on its back. She screamed for help as loud as she could, but seconds later the beast dove beneath the waves and carried her off to its realm in the deep.

Luckily, some of the people in the wife's village heard her screams, and they ran to Gunarhnesemgyet and told him what had happened. They were truly sorry for him, one of them said, for his loving wife had gone to an untimely rest in the land of the monsters, never to return. If there was anything his neighbors could do to console him, he should not hesitate to ask. Gunarhnesemgyet immediately began gathering his hunting weapons and headed for his canoe while the villagers followed along. What was he doing? they anxiously asked. Surely he did not intend to follow the monster to its horrible homeland, for if he did so he would surely be eaten alive, just like his unfortunate wife!

The hunter told the people to stop their cowardly talk and climbed into his canoe. His wife was still alive, he insisted. He could not explain how he knew this. Perhaps, he suggested, it was the great bond he and his wife were blessed to share, for the two truly believed that their souls were forever intertwined and could not be separated. His soul could not thrive without hers, he said, and that was why he had to go after her and either save her or die with her. The villagers continued to argue against his seemingly rash decision, but he ignored them and with determined strokes paddled the boat out to sea.

In the House of the Monster-King

When Gunarhnesemgyet reached the spot where the monster had disappeared under the surface with his wife, he tied a long leather string to his canoe. Then, holding the other end of the string, he dove into the water and swam downward

The Awesome Thunderbird

Although most of the monstrous beings in Native American mythology are evil or destructive, a few are better described as aloof and awe inspiring. Perhaps the most obvious example is the Thunderbird, recognized in one form or another by almost every North American tribe. Scholar Philip Wilkinson describes the Thunderbird in *The Illustrated Dictionary of Mythology*.

Almost every North American tribe recognized the Thunderbird, pictured here.

Feared all over North America, the Thunderbird is like an enormous eagle that can swoop down from the sky and carry away any living creature—even something as enormous as a whale. The flash when he blinks his eyes makes lightning, and the thunder is caused by the beating of his wings. Sometimes he travels around with a pair of lightning serpents, which are said to transform themselves into his belt and his harpoon. Although the bird is dangerous, with the power to cause rapid death, many people believe that seeing or hearing the Thunderbird is a sign of good luck or forthcoming wealth.

For these reasons, many tribes carved totems and other figurines of the Thunderbird, especially the peoples who inhabited the plains of the American Midwest.

until he reached the bottom. There, to his surprise, he found himself in a grove of trees not unlike those in his own world. He was also astonished to find that there was air on the sea bottom, so he was able to breathe normally.

Before long, the hunter came to a village inhabited by beings that were half human and half bird. They were also blind because the skin of their eyelids had grown together, obscuring their vision. Gunarhnesemgyet told them that he was looking for a human woman held captive by a monster. He realized that they were blind and could not actually have seen either the woman or the monster, but perhaps they might have heard them go by. Any clue, no matter how small, might help the hunter determine the direction in which they had gone.

After a few seconds one of the bird-men stepped forward. The woman and the monster had in fact passed by this place, he said, and not very long ago. But if the bird-men told the man the direction to go, what would they receive in return? Gunarhnesemgyet thought about it for a moment and then unsheathed his knife and cut open the eyelids of the bird-men, allowing them to see. They were so grateful to him that they gave him explicit directions for finding the great house where the king of the sea monsters dwelled. The hunter's wife was almost certainly a prisoner there, they told him. What is more, because of her unusual beauty the monster-king would likely not eat her. Instead, he would use his potent magic to change her into a sea creature and then mate with her.

Horrified by the prospect of the love of his life becoming a hideous monster, Gunarhnesemgyet hurried along the path the bird-men had told him to follow. Soon he came to the great house of the monster-king. Carefully sneaking up to a window and peering in, he saw his wife, her hands bound, sitting in the midst of a large group of monsters. Some of them were females who were waiting on the biggest creature of all; Gunarhnesemgyet reasoned these were the monster-king and its wives. He hastily devised a clever rescue plan. Taking a bucket that lay near the front door, he filled it with water, then burst into the lodge and threw the water onto the fire in the central hearth. The late British Museum scholar Cottie Burland told what happened next:

> Steam gushed from the fire and the house was filled with white mist. In the confusion, Gunarhnesemgyet rushed to his wife, crying, "Come escape!" They made for the door. [After exiting the house,] Gunarhnesemgyet put some magical medicine in his mouth and blew it toward the king of the monsters. The king gradually began to swell, until he became so huge that he blocked the door. In an attempt to shrink him, his wives rushed over and urinated on him, but the shrinking was slow and it was some time

before the monsters could pass through the door. Thus, Gunarhnesemgyet had a chance to escape with his wife.[32]

By the time the monsters began their pursuit, the escaping couple had reached the string that the hunter had earlier and very wisely attached to the canoe. Gunarhnesemgyet and his wife used the string to pull themselves up, climbed into the boat, and paddled back to their village before the sea monsters could catch up. In this way, two humans visited the monsters' realm and lived to tell about it; and the souls of the two lovers were reunited, never to be separated again.

The Nightmare That Came True

Many monsters existed on land, too, of course. Among these were the frightful human heads that, for one reason or another, had been disconnected from their bodies. These heads roamed around by various means, sometimes rolling along the ground, other times bouncing up and down like balls, and still other times floating through the air on the winds or by magic. Almost always the heads were evil or demented or both. And many were cannibalistic, hunting down innocent people and devouring them, either dead or alive.

One of the more bizarre and unsettling Native American tales of monstrous heads concerns a warrior who lived in the forests of California. The warrior had heard about heads that rolled around in the night searching for victims to eat. And such tales gave him goose bumps and sent shivers down his spine. He told his fourteen-year-old son that if he ever saw one of those ghastly bodiless heads, he should kill it immediately; he should smash it with a rock or stab it with his lance. Whatever he did, he must not let the head bite him, for supposedly the saliva of such monsters could make a person sleepy. And if the boy were to fall asleep before the thing were dead, it might devour him! The son, who got goose bumps as large as his father's from thinking about the terrible heads, agreed to do as his father said.

Little did the boy know that he would soon have occasion to test how well he followed his father's instructions. That very night, the warrior had a nightmare in which he ate up his own body, turning himself into one of the very monster heads he dreaded. After waking up in a sweat, the man could not get back to sleep. In the morning, after breakfast, father and son went out into the forest to gather pine nuts. Following their usual procedure, the boy climbed up a pine tree and harvested the large seeds, then tossed them down to his father, who put them in a basket. Everything was going smoothly, but suddenly one of the nuts the son was holding slipped from his grasp. It fell downward, gaining momentum, and struck his father on the hand, opening a small cut. The man cried out in pain and told the boy to try to be a little more care-

The Giant Worm

Another kind of monster described in Native American myths takes the form of a huge serpent or worm, in many ways similar to a category of monster common in Norse and Chinese myths. In this excerpt from his informative book *North American Indian Mythology*, the late Cottie Burland, one of the leading scholars in the field during the twentieth century, tells the story of one such monstrous worm. In a novel twist, the usual roles are reversed, with the monster becoming the victim and eliciting sympathy.

A chief's daughter had a woodworm for a pet. She fed it with her own milk and as it grew bigger she took food for it from the store-boxes of her parents. When it was two fathoms long,

The monstrous serpent, Avan Yu, thought to dwell under the earth.

she made up a cradle song for it, "You have a face already and can sit up." . . . [Hearing the girl repeat the song many times over the course of several months, her mother wondered who she was singing to] and peeped into the hut where [the girl spent much of her time] . . . and saw the enormous worm. The people in the village were frightened, especially as some of them had noticed that the boxes in which they stored oil supplies for winter food had been emptied by some creature that tunneled in underneath the ground. They blamed the worm. The chief tried to persuade his daughter to come out of the . . . hut and, knowing that she could not disobey, she changed her song to a mourning song for the worm and returned to her father's house. As soon as she had gone, the villagers attacked the worm and cut it in pieces. The starvation that threatened them through the loss of their oil supplies was soon averted by good fortune and fishing. The girl explained that the tribe's success was due to the spirit of the worm.

ful. The son apologized and assured the father that it would not happen again.

Then something very strange and repulsive happened. When the warrior licked his hand to stop the bleeding, he was suddenly gripped by an odd and irresistible desire to taste more blood. He bit into his hand, tearing out a large hunk of flesh, and swallowed the hideous morsel. Though he tried to stop himself from taking more bites from his own body, he could not resist the compulsion that had taken possession of him. As his son watched in horror from up above, the warrior devoured his own arm and then continued biting and chewing until there was nothing left of him but a head rolling on the ground. Incredibly, and for reasons that no one could explain, the man's nightmare had come true! At this frightening moment, the boy remembered what his father had told him to do if he should ever encounter a monster head. But though the young boy was terrified and disgusted by what he saw, he could not bring himself to destroy the head, for it was, after all, an important piece of his own father.

Meanwhile, the head did not wait around. Consumed by an overwhelming need for blood and flesh, the thing bounced around the forest looking for victims. Eventually, the son came to his senses and realized that it would be best

A modern painting depicts a Sioux warrior taking aim at a giant rattlesnake, a Native American monster popular in the west and southwest.

for everyone, including his father, to destroy the head. Aided by ten of the village's best hunters, he tracked down the monster, which bounced around frantically in an attempt to get away. The head must have become so crazed with fear that it did not see where it was going; it ended up bouncing off an embankment and into the local river. There, the son and the hunters watched as the head drowned and sank to the bottom. Thereafter, everyone in the village got goose bumps when they thought about the boy's father, and all kept a watchful eye for strange round objects rolling around in the night.

The foregoing tales of heroes grappling with sea monsters and of monstrous heads menacing society illustrate both the wide diversity of Native American mythical monsters and the common thread running through their stories. On the one hand, sea monsters and disembodied heads are very different kinds of monsters. One lives in the water, the other on land; one gets around by swimming, the other by rolling or bouncing; one is a whole being, but the other is not. As dissimilar as these monsters are, however, they were both pictured frequently in the myths of tribes living far from one another and having little or no direct contact. How certain core elements of these tales slowly spread across the continent continues to be of interest to scholars, and these colorful, enduring stories remain one of the crucial cultural ties uniting American Indians from Maine to California.

Notes

Introduction—The Dragons of the Past

1. Max J. Herzberg, *Myths and Their Meanings*. Boston: Allyn and Bacon, n.d., p. 2.
2. Edith Hamilton, *Mythology*. New York: New American Library, 1940, p. 19.
3. Carl Sagan, *The Dragons of Eden*. New York: Ballantine Books, 1977, pp. 150–51.

Chapter One—Ancient Greece: The Beast with a Woman's Face

4. Hesiod, *Theogony*, in *Hesiod and Theognis*. Trans. Dorothea Wender. New York: Penguin Books, 1973, p. 42.
5. Semonides, *On Women*, in Mary R. Lefkowitz and Maureen B. Fant, eds., *Women's Life in Greece and Rome: A Source Book in Translation*. Baltimore: Johns Hopkins University Press, 1992, p. 27.
6. Diodorus Siculus, *Library of History*, in Rhoda A. Hendricks, trans., *Classical Gods and Heroes: Myths as Told by the Ancient Authors*. New York: Morrow Quill, 1974, p. 108.
7. That happiness eventually came to an abrupt end, however. Oedipus discovered that his wife, Jocasta, was actually his mother. Moreover, a man he had killed in self-defense on the roadside on his way to Thebes was none other than Laius, Jocasta's former husband and his real father. Polybus, the man Oedipus had sought to protect by leaving Corinth, had taken in the infant Oedipus after he had been abandoned by Laius and Jocasta. Thus, the oracle's terrible prediction had come true, despite Oedipus's attempts to subvert it.
8. David Bellingham, *An Introduction to Greek Mythology*. Secaucus, NJ: Chartwell Books, 1989, p. 83.
9. Ovid, *Metamorphoses*. Trans. Horace Gregory. New York: New American Library, 1958, p. 134.
10. Apollonius of Rhodes, *Argonautica,* published as *The Voyage of the* Argo. Trans. E. V. Rieu. New York: Penguin Books, 1971, p. 80.

Chapter Two—Ancient Persia: The Battle Between Good and Evil

11. Quoted in Vesta S. Curtis, *Persian Myths*. Austin: University of Texas Press, 1993, p. 23.
12. John R. Hinnells, *Persian Mythology*. New York: Peter Bedrick Books, 1985, pp. 42–44.
13. Firdausi, *Shahnameh*, in A. Berriedale Keith and Albert J. Carnoy, *The Mythology of All Races*, vol. 6, *Indian and Iranian*. New York: Cooper Square, 1964, p. 310.
14. Quoted in Curtis, *Persian Myths*, p. 34.
15. Norma L. Goodrich, *Ancient Myths*. New York: New American Library, 1960, pp. 133–34.
16. Quoted in Curtis, *Persian Myths*, p. 38.

Chapter Three—Ancient India: Demonic Enemies of Gods and Humans

17. Veronica Ions, *Indian Mythology*. New York: Peter Bedrick Books, 1984, pp. 112–13.
18. Quoted in Keith and Carnoy, *The Mythology of All Races*, p. 46.
19. Ions, *Indian Mythology*, p. 116.

20. Elizabeth Seeger, ed., *The Ramayana*. New York: William R. Scott, 1969, p. 106.
21. Quoted in Seeger, *The Ramayana*, p. 118.
22. Seeger, *The Ramayana*, pp. 212–13.

Chapter Four—Ancient Africa: Shape-Shifters, Imps, and River Monsters

23. Geoffrey Parrinder, *African Mythology*. New York: Peter Bedrick Books, 1986, pp. 93–94.

Chapter Five—Ancient Scandinavia: Dragons and Giants in a Bleak World

24. Hamilton, *Mythology*, p. 300.
25. H. R. Ellis Davidson, *Scandinavian Mythology*. New York: Peter Bedrick Books, 1986, p. 8.
26. Davidson, *Scandinavian Mythology*, pp. 161–62.
27. Saxo's history is also the original source of the story of a Danish prince and his family troubles, which William Shakespeare later adapted for his most famous play—*Hamlet*.
28. H. R. Ellis Davidson, *Gods and Myths of Northern Europe*. Baltimore: Penguin Books, 1964, p. 41.
29. Philip Wilkinson, *The Illustrated Dictionary of Mythology*. New York: Dorling Kindersley, 1998, p. 84.

Chapter Six—Ancient North America: In the Belly of the Sea Monster

30. Hartley B. Alexander, *The Mythology of All Races*, vol. 10, *North American*. New York: Cooper Square, 1964, p. 268.
31. Alexander, *The Mythology of All Races*, p. 274.
32. Cottie Burland, *North American Indian Mythology*. Rev. Marion Wood. New York: Peter Bedrick Books, 1985, p. 45.

For Further Reading

Joyce C. Arkhurst, *The Adventures of Spider: West African Folktales*. Boston: Little, Brown, 1992. A charming, nicely illustrated collection of African myths that serves as a nice introduction to the larger, more complex subject of African mythology.

David Bellingham, *An Introduction to Greek Mythology*. Secaucus, NJ: Chartwell Books, 1989. Explains the major Greek myths and legends and their importance to the ancient Greeks. Contains many beautiful photos and drawings.

Richard Erdoes and Alfonso Ortiz, eds., *American Indian Myths and Legends*. New York: Pantheon Books, 1985. Dozens of entertaining Native American tales are included in this well-written volume.

Charles Kingsley, *The Heroes*. Santa Rosa, CA: Classics, 1968. This is a reprint of the original book by Kingsley, the renowned nineteenth-century social reformer, university professor, and classical scholar, a work he wrote for his three children. Contains his superb retellings of the stories of Jason, Perseus, Theseus, and Heracles.

Mary P. Osborne, *Favorite Norse Myths*. New York: Scholastic, 1996. A handsomely illustrated compilation of Norse myths, including stories involving monsters, giants, and dwarves.

Neil Philip, *The Illustrated Book of Myths: Tales and Legends of the World*. New York: Dorling Kindersley, 1995. An excellent introduction to world mythology for young people, enlivened with many stunning photos and drawings.

———, *Mythology*. New York: Knopf, 1999. Another fine beginners' mythology volume by Philip, who has written a number of other children's books on the subject, including *Fairy Tales of Eastern Europe* and *The Arabian Nights*.

Charles Phillips et al., *The Eternal Cycle: Indian Myth*. New York: Time-Life Books, 2000. A commendable introduction to the Buddhist, Hindu, and other myths of India. Like other Time-Life volumes, this one contains a number of colorful and appropriate illustrations.

Works Consulted

Thomas Bulfinch, *Bulfinch's Mythology*. New York: Dell, 1959. This is one of several versions of this well-known and useful work, which is itself a modern compilation of two of Bulfinch's original books—*The Age of Fable* (1855), a retelling of the Greek and Roman myths, and *The Age of Chivalry* (1858), an account of the Arthurian legends.

Cottie Burland, *North American Indian Mythology*. Rev. Marion Wood. New York: Peter Bedrick Books, 1985. This volume, by the late Cottie Burland, a scholar at the British Museum and an authority on Native American myths, is divided according to geographical regions, such as "Hunters of the Northern Forests," "Farmers of the Eastern Woodlands," and "Dwellers on the Mesas."

Vesta S. Curtis, *Persian Myths*. Austin: University of Texas Press, 1993. This is a brief but well-written and authoritative synopsis and analysis of the characters and themes of Persian/Iranian mythology.

H. R. Ellis Davidson, *Gods and Myths of Northern Europe*. Baltimore: Penguin Books, 1964. This is one of the best general overviews of Norse mythology, written by one of the acknowledged experts in the field.

———, *Scandinavian Mythology*. New York: Peter Bedrick Books, 1986. Another excellent overview of Norse myths, this one is beautifully illustrated with many photos of Scandinavian vistas and Norse artifacts.

Mircea Eliade, ed., *Essential Sacred Writings from Around the World*. San Francisco: Harper Collins, 1967. A massive, useful volume containing excerpts from the actual surviving religious texts and stories of ancient Africa, North America, India, Europe, and elsewhere.

Michael Grant, *Myths of the Greeks and Romans*. New York: New American Library, 1962. One of the twentieth century's most prolific and respected classical historians here delivers a fine rendition of the important Greek and Roman myths, along with plenty of background information and analysis.

Edith Hamilton, *Mythology*. New York: New American Library, 1940. Hamilton's excellent retelling of the Greek myths is still considered by many to be the best and most entertaining overview of its kind.

Rhoda A. Hendricks, trans., *Classical Gods and Heroes: Myths as Told by the Ancient Authors*. New York: Morrow Quill, 1974. A collection of easy-to-read translations of famous Greek myths and tales, as told by ancient Greek and Roman writers, including Homer, Hesiod, Pindar, Apollodorus, Ovid, and Virgil.

John R. Hinnells, *Persian Mythology*. New York: Peter Bedrick Books, 1985.

Hinnells, a Manchester University scholar, presents a comprehensive, enlightening summary of ancient Persian mythology, devoting the bulk of his discussion to Zoroastrian characters and stories (which incorporated characters and themes from older Iranian myths).

Veronica Ions, *Indian Mythology*. New York: Peter Bedrick Books, 1984. This volume by Ions, a scholar who has written several other widely read books about mythology, is a well-written summary of a complex and highly detailed subject.

Geoffrey Parrinder, *African Mythology*. New York: Peter Bedrick Books, 1986. Parrinder, who teaches comparative religions at the University of London, has done an admirable job of surveying the complex web of folklore from the many separate peoples of the African continent, a portion of world mythology that is often overlooked in the educational curricula of Western countries. He breaks down his chapters rather conveniently by theme, for example, "The Creator," "The Mystery of Birth," "Gods and Spirits," "Witches and Monsters," and so forth.

Philip Wilkinson, *The Illustrated Dictionary of Mythology*. New York: Dorling Kindersley, 1998. This well-written, handsomely mounted book contains short overviews of hundreds of mythological characters, facts, and stories of peoples from around the world.

Additional Works Consulted

Hartley B. Alexander, *The Mythology of All Races*. Vol. 10. *North American*. New York: Cooper Square, 1964.

Apollonius of Rhodes, *Argonautica*, published as *The Voyage of the* Argo. Trans. E. V. Rieu. New York: Penguin Books, 1971.

Henry A. Bellows, trans., *The Poetic Edda*. New York: American-Scandinavian Foundation, 1923.

C. M. Bowra, *The Greek Experience*. New York: New American Library, 1957.

Mary Boyce, ed. and trans., *Textual Sources for the Study of Zoroastrianism*. Totowa, NJ: Barnes and Noble, 1984.

Joseph Campbell, *Myths to Live By*. New York: Bantam Books, 1972.

Peter Connolly, *The Legend of Odysseus*. New York: Oxford University Press, 1986.

John Curtis, *Ancient Persia*. Cambridge, MA: Harvard University Press, 1990.

H. Byron Earhart, ed., *Religious Traditions of the World*. San Francisco: HarperCollins, 1993.

Eerdmans' Handbook to the World's Religions. Grand Rapids, MI: William B. Eerdmans, 1982.

Charles Freeman, *The Greek Achievement: The Foundation of the Western World*. New York: Viking/Penguin, 1999.

Norma L. Goodrich, *Ancient Myths*. New York: New American Library, 1960.

Max J. Herzberg, *Myths and Their Meanings*. Boston: Allyn and Bacon, n.d.

Hesiod, *Theogony*, in *Hesiod and Theognis*. Trans. Dorothea Wender. New York: Penguin Books, 1973.

Frederick E. Hoxie, ed., *Encyclopedia of North American Indians*. New York: Houghton Mifflin, 1996.

Alvin M. Josephy Jr., ed., *The Horizon History of Africa*. New York: McGraw-Hill, 1971.

A. Berriedale Keith and Albert J. Carnoy, *The Mythology of All Races*, Vol. 6, *Indian and Iranian*. New York: Cooper Square, 1964.

Mary R. Lefkowitz and Maureen B. Fant, eds., *Women's Life in Greece and Rome: A Source Book in Translation*. Baltimore: Johns Hopkins University Press, 1992.

A. A. Macdonell, *A Vedic Reader for Students*. Oxford: Clarendon, 1917.

Mark P. O. Morford and Robert J. Lenardon, *Classical Mythology*. New York: Longman, 1985.

Ovid, *Metamorphoses*. Trans. Horace Gregory. New York: New American Library, 1958.

John G. Pedley, *Greek Art and Archaeology*. New York: Harry N. Abrams, 1993.

John Pinsent, *Greek Mythology*. New York: Peter Bedrick Books, 1986.

James B. Pritchard, ed., *Ancient Near Eastern Texts Relating to the Old Testament*. Princeton, NJ: Princeton University Press, 1969.

W. H. D. Rouse, *Gods, Heroes, and Men of Ancient Greece*. New York: New American Library, 1957.

Carl Sagan, *The Dragons of Eden*. New York: Ballantine Books, 1977.

Elizabeth Seeger, ed., *The Ramayana*. New York: William R. Scott, 1969.

Carl Waldman, *Atlas of the North American Indian*. New York: Facts On File, 1985.

Index

Picture Credits

About the Author

Historian Don Nardo has written several volumes about ancient cultures and their religious beliefs and mythologies, among them *Life in Ancient Athens*, *The Persian Empire*, *Greek and Roman Mythology*, and *Egyptian Mythology*. Mr. Nardo is also the editor of Greenhaven Press's massive *Complete History of Ancient Greece*. He lives with his wife, Christine, in Massachusetts.